Financialization and the US Economy

NEW DIRECTIONS IN MODERN ECONOMICS

Series Editor: Malcolm C. Sawyer, *Professor of Economics, University of Leeds, UK*

New Directions in Modern Economics presents a challenge to orthodox economic thinking. It focuses on new ideas emanating from radical traditions including post-Keynesian, Kaleckian, neo-Ricardian and Marxian. The books in the series do not adhere rigidly to any single school of thought but attempt to present a positive alternative to the conventional wisdom.

A list of published titles in this series is printed at the end of this volume.

Financialization and the US Economy

Özgür Orhangazi

Roosevelt University, USA

NEW DIRECTIONS IN MODERN ECONOMICS

Edward Elgar

Cheltenham, UK • Northampton, MA, USA

© Özgür Orhangazi, 2008

ᴍᴄ

Published by
Edward Elgar Publishing Limited
Glensanda House
Montpellier Parade
Cheltenham
Glos GL50 1UA
UK

Edward Elgar Publishing, Inc.
William Pratt House
9 Dewey Court
Northampton
Massachusetts 01060
USA

A catalogue record for this book
is available from the British Library

Library of Congress Cataloging in Publication Data

Orhangazi, Özgür, 1977–
    Financialization and the US economy / Özgür Orhangazi.
        p. cm. — (New directions in modern economics series)
    Includes bibliographical references and index.
    1. Finance—United States. 2. Financial services industry—United States.
    3. United States—Economic conditions—2001– I. Title.
    HG181.O74 2007
    332.10973—dc22

                                                              2007032320

ISBN 978 1 84720 594 0

Printed and bound in Great Britain by MPG Books Ltd, Bodmin, Cornwall

Contents

Figures

Tables

Abbreviations

BEA	Bureau of Economic Analysis
CEO	chief executive officer
FCC	Ford Credit Company
FDIC	Federal Deposit Insurance Corporation
FED	Federal Reserve
FIRE	finance, insurance and real estate
FFA	Flow of Funds Accounts
GDP	Gross Domestic Product
GMAC	General Motors Acceptance Corporation
GSE	Government Sponsored Enterprise
IMF	International Monetary Fund
IRS	Internal Revenue Service
NAICS	North American Industry Classification System
NASDAQ	National Association of Securities Dealers Automated Quotations
NIPA	National Income and Product Accounts
NFC	nonfinancial corporation
NYSE	New York Stock Exchange
OECD	Organisation for Economic Co-operation and Development
OTC	over-the-counter
SIC	Standard Industry Classification
GMM	Generalized Method of Moments

Foreword

The financial collapse that began in the US in 1929 and the ensuing Great Depression to which it contributed, convinced the government, the public and much of the business class that a lightly regulated financial system free to pursue the parochial interests of its practitioners would inevitably lead to financial crises, some of which could create serious economic distress. In the case of the 1930s, the collapse threatened the economic and political viability of the country. The public blamed the Depression on greedy and powerful financial forces, perhaps to an unwarranted degree. Fear of the dangers of an unleashed financial system led to the adoption in the 1930s and 1940s of the strongest system of financial regulation the country ever experienced.

In the so-called 'Golden Age of Modern Capitalism' which lasted from about 1950 through the early 1970s, the appropriate role for the financial sector was thought to be as the 'servant' of the real sector rather than its pre-1930s role as its 'master.' This servant role was assured by strong financial regulation. Under government guidance, financial markets provided low-cost funds for business investment and for home building as well as a secure haven for household savings. And regulation minimized the likelihood of speculative financial booms and crises – while about 9000 banks failed in the 1930s, there were virtually no bank failures in these decades. The positive role played by the financial system was thought to have made a strong contribution to the best economic performance in US history in this era.

A series of events that took place after the late 1960s gravely weakened the Golden Age financial regime. These include the breakdown of the Bretton Woods fixed exchange rate system in the early 1970s, two bursts of inflation triggered by oil price shocks in the mid- and late-1970s that wreaked havoc on a regulatory system unprepared to deal with high inflation, and the Latin American debt crisis that threatened the solvency of large US money center banks in the 1980s. The stress these developments placed on the regulatory system, combined with an incessant demand for regulatory relief by increasingly politically influential financial interests, and an erosion of belief in the efficacy of regulation by those charged with enforcing the rules, eventually led to its dismantling. The new approach to regulation was based on the belief that free financial markets with only the lightest touch of regulatory restraint will produce optimal outcomes. Alan Greenspan, considered the 'wisest' of financial market observers and, as Chairman of the Federal Reserve Board of Governors, the top regulator of US financial markets from 1987 through 2005, said recently that he 'didn't get involved in regulatory matters in part because his laissez-faire philosophy was often at odds with the goals of the laws Congress had tasked the Fed with enforcing' (*Wall Street Journal*, 'Did Greenspan add to subprime woes?', 9 June 2007).

As the Golden Age financial regulation system was unraveling, financial markets grew at astonishing speed. The rapid increase in pension funds and institutional investors, coupled with recycled petro dollars and, after 1980, rising capital inflows to the US, provided vast supplies of funds to financial markets. Meanwhile, the demand for credit was fed by rising government budget deficits, an increased demand for home mortgages, the hostile takeover movement of the 1980s (followed after 2001 by the boom in private equity leveraged buyouts), and by the credit needs of financial institutions themselves in a process known as 'financial deepening.' Credit market debt grew from about 150 percent of GDP in the period from 1960 to 1980 to more than 300 percent by 2003. Total financial assets had been less than 500 percent of GDP from 1960 to 1980, but were over 900 percent by 2003. Released from their regulatory chains, financial markets did what they always seem to do when left to themselves: they exploded in size and became more volatile.

In the first decade or so after the demise of the Golden Age, US financial market growth took place in an environment in which the rules of the game set by regulators were changing dramatically and market conditions were volatile. It is thus not surprising that the overall profitability of the financial sector was itself volatile and disappointing in the 1980s. Financial sector profits cycled around 1.5 percent of GDP from 1960 to the late 1970s, but fell to below 1 percent in the mid-1980s. They began to rise rapidly in the early 1990s and by the early 2000s were over 3 percent of GDP. Thus, since the early 1990s the US has had a lightly regulated but very profitable financial system growing at rates far beyond those of the real sector. The gross value added of financial corporations rose from about 6 percent of nonfinancial corporate gross value added in the 1960s to 16 percent in the early 2000s. The current conventional wisdom is that financial markets should be the mechanism that decides how to allocate real resources to their most efficient uses – the brain of the system and once again the 'master' of the real sector.

Of course the US economy was not the only one to experience a 'free market' financial transformation; the US quickly began exporting the new model around the world. Indeed, the deregulation of domestic financial systems and the deconstruction of barriers to the cross-border movement of money was a central mechanism in the process that spread neoliberalism around the world. It was the collapse of the US banking system in the early 1980s that led to the imposition of 'Washington Consensus' restructuring policies across much of Latin America. Many 'developing' countries, under pressure from Western governments, multinational banks and international financial institutions, loosened controls over inward capital flows. A rush of hot money often flowed into these countries, causing speculative bubbles. When these bubbles burst, money flowed out again, causing currency and financial crises. The G-8 countries, the IMF and the World Bank would then offer foreign currency loans needed to overcome the crisis, but only if affected governments agreed to more fully open their economies to foreign capital, impose restrictive macro policy and adopt 'structural adjustment' to convert the economy to a neoliberal model. Demands to allow foreign financial institutions untrammeled access to the domestic economy were usually the most vigorously pursued. Thus, the dramatic increase in the size and influence of global financial markets has been coterminous with and constitutive of the spread of neoliberalism across the globe. It is hard to analyse one in isolation from the other.

Eventually, most countries adopted lightly regulated, globally integrated financial markets. These markets eventually became more powerful in their effects on economic activity than at any time since J.P. Morgan's 'Money Trust' dominated the US economy in the decades before the Great Depression. Since the distribution of ownership of financial wealth among households is now so concentrated, the average returns to financial wealth have been so high, and compensation for top executives has reached gargantuan levels, income and wealth inequality has skyrocketed everywhere. Financial asset price volatility has increased, making financial investment by ordinary families riskier just when the decline of traditional pension plans makes them more dependent on financial assets to fund their retirements. Financial innovations such as derivatives have raised qualitatively the complexity and non-transparency of financial markets even as they have become more powerful and moved beyond effective government control.

With this brief description of the evolution of financial markets, we can assess the contributions to our understanding of the complex effects of finance on economic activity contained in Özgür Orhangazi's book *Financialization and the US Economy*. This book should be of interest to the general reader, who simply wants to learn more about the causes and effects of the transformation of financial markets, and it contains important new empirical evidence about the effects of financial change on nonfinancial corporate behavior that should be of interest to academic scholars working in this area as well as government and business leaders concerned about the future of the US economy and the well-being of the majority of Americans.

The general reader will find the first five chapters quite informative. In the opening chapter, Orhangazi discusses 'financialization,' a term meant to capture the complex set of relations between financial markets and other aspects of the economy. There are many definitions of this elastic term in the literature. Consider one: 'the increasing role of financial motives, financial markets, financial actors and financial institutions in the operation of the domestic and international economy' – a complex concept indeed. He accepts a broad definition of financialization at 'the general level' to guide his review of the literature, but when he moves to statistical hypothesis testing in the latter part of the book, he defines financialization more narrowly as 'changes in the relationship between the nonfinancial corporate sector and financial markets.' The second chapter documents empirically the rapid growth of financial markets, financial firms and financial assets relative to the rest of the economy. The third chapter presents an overview of the evolution of the US financial system from the rise of what is often called 'Finance Capital' around the turn of the last century to the current period. In the section on Morgan's 'Money Trust,' Orhangazi astutely notes one important difference between the relation of financial to nonfinancial sectors of the economy then and now. Then, the most powerful bankers held direct control over many of the most important firms and industries in the country and cooperated to bring order and rationality to industries previously wracked by destructive competition, cutthroat pricing and chronic excess capacity. Today, powerful financial institutions have neither the means nor the desire to impose rationality on the economic system as a whole. Rather, they pursue their individual interests via speculation and risk-taking, capitalizing on information asymmetries (sellers of complex financial products always know more than buyers about these products), and through constant innovation that creates niche markets with high but temporary profit margins as it feeds market volatility.

Chapter 4 contains an insightful review of the literature on financialization. Orhangazi organizes the abundance of articles and books on this diverse subject into three categories: first, literature that sees the current dominance of finance as one phase of a repeating long wave in the history of capitalism; second, works that understand the rise of finance in the past 30 years as tightly connected to, and an integral part of, the rise of the global neoliberal order; third, writings which focus on the effects of financial markets on the governance and performance of nonfinancial firms in the current era – his own area of specialization. This review is especially useful because it critically evaluates as well as summarizes arguments put forth by various authors.

The last section of Chapter 4 provides a point of entry into the last three substantive chapters of the book, which will be of special interest to those already familiar with these issues. The focus of these chapters is the impact of today's financial markets on the capital investment decisions of non-financial corporations in the US. In the Golden Age, it is argued, the US relied on the dominant real-sector 'managerial firm' to guide the economy over time. These firms made strategic decisions, including those affecting capital investment, based on their projected impact on the long-term growth and prosperity of the enterprise, and funded most investment projects with 'patient' sources of finance – mostly internal funds. Firms could also sell long-term bonds at modest real rates of interest. Equity holders typically held their shares for long periods, leaving management free of short-term stock market pressure. Real sector firms guided the economy; financial markets assisted in their efforts. Capital investment grew rapidly, helping sustain equally rapid productivity growth.

Everything in this picture changed dramatically in the past three decades. Average real interest rates have been much higher than before. Both the planning horizon and the objectives of managers of large nonfinancial firms have changed. The hostile takeover movement of the 1980s punished managers whose companies had low stock prices; they thus either had to raise their stock price in the short run by actions detrimental to the firm's long-term health (such as borrowing to pay dividends or finance stock buy-backs) or lose control of their companies to outsiders. In the 1990s, these firms began to compensate their most important executives with lavish stock options to harmonize their personal incentives with the objective of their institutional investors – to maximize stock price gains in the short run. In the present decade, both of these forces are at work: private equity funds threaten to take over firms with low stock prices while corporate executives' compensation is based largely on stock options. Moreover, as Orhangazi demonstrates, companies now disgorge a much higher percent of their cash flow back to financial markets in the form of stock buybacks and interest and dividend payments than they did in the Golden Age. While they can always go back to the market to try and re-borrow these funds, this process of 'impatient finance' creates uncertainty about the cost and availability of investment funding and, again, induces a shorter planning horizon. Finally, through much of the new era, the rate of return that could be earned by nonfinancial corporations through investment in financial assets and/or in financial subsidiaries exceeded the rate of return on capital investment. This induced firms to substitute financial for real investment. All these factors – short planning horizons, expensive and uncertain access to external funds, pursuit of short-term stock price gains rather than long-term growth, and attractive alternatives to capital investment offered in financial markets – are believed to have exerted downward pressure on capital spending.

All these assertions receive empirical support in the financialization literature through the use of institutional analysis, case studies and the examination of the movement of relevant variables over time. The conclusion that the rate of growth of investment in the neoliberal era is slower than it was in the Golden Age is also evident in the data. Unfortunately, very few scholars have attempted to formally test the effects of these changes on investment spending using up-to-date statistical techniques. However, in Chapter 6, Orhangazi uses time series regression methods to test two key 'financialization' hypotheses using aggregate data for US nonfinancial corporations: that payments to financial markets restrict capital investment because external funds are either more expensive than internal funds or have quantity constraints; and that profits from financial investments lower capital investment even though they expand internal funds because they signal the superiority of financial investment opportunities. He finds that, *ceteris paribus*, capital investment spending is reduced as payments to financial markets increase and as profits from financial investment rise. In mainstream economic theory, an increase in either these variables should not restrict investment. However, while both variables have the posited sign, the coefficient on the financial payments variable is statistically significant only at the 10 percent level, while the coefficient on the financial profits variable is not statistically significant.

Orhangazi is aware that econometric tests on aggregations of disparate firms can lead to both misleading results as well as low coefficient estimation precision. An aggregate regression might conclude, for example, that financial payments have no effect on investment only because half the firms in the sample react positively and significantly to an increase in this variable while the other half responds negatively. Each effect cancels the other, leading the researcher unaware of the importance of financialization on key economic sectors and thus unable to investigate why some firms are adversely affected by financial markets while others are not. To overcome this problem, in Chapter 7 he analyses the effects of his two 'financialization' variables on capital investment spending from 1973–2003 using panel data taken from Standard and Poor's Compustat firm data set. With this micro data, he tests his hypotheses using all the nonfinancial firms in the set, but he also runs separate regressions on firms of different size and firms in different industries. The use of micro data allows Orhangazi to test a much richer set of hypotheses than is possible under the restrictions of macro data sets. To take two important examples, he finds that the financial payments variable has negative and statistically significant coefficients in almost all regressions, and that the financial profits variable has negative and significant coefficients for larger firms – which are precisely the firms for which we would expect impediments to investment spending from the 'financialization' pressures described above to be most severe.

As far as I know, this is the first study to subject important hypotheses about the effects of financialization on corporate investment to econometric testing using a micro data set. It thus provides the most convincing statistical evidence yet that modern financial markets constrain rather than facilitate robust capital investment. The combination of this empirical contribution and the insightful review of and commentary on the financialization literature in the early chapters makes this book well worth reading.

15 June 2007

James Crotty
Sheridan Scholar and Professor of Economics
University of Massachusetts Amherst

Acknowledgements

This book is a revised and updated version of the Ph.D. thesis that I completed at the University of Massachusetts Amherst in September 2006. I would like to thank Bob Pollin for his help and encouragement in preparing this work for publication. I received assistance and support from many people in completing the original dissertation. Jim Crotty has provided guidance from the very beginning of the project and contributed to it in many ways. I owe a great debt to Jim for all his contributions. Bob Pollin, Léonce Ndikumana and James Heintz, have offered valuable suggestions and comments throughout the research and writing stages. I am grateful to Michael Ash, Mark Brenner, Geert Dhondt, Mathieu Dufour, Gerald Epstein, Armağan Gezici, Arjun Jayadev, David Kotz, Gökçer Özgür, Elizabeth Ramey and Peter Skott for their insightful comments and precious help. Of course, any shortcomings in this work are my own responsibility. I would also like to thank Bob Pickens and Alan Sturmer at Edward Elgar for being very helpful in preparing the text for publication. Finally, special thanks go to Devrim for all her direct and indirect support and more importantly, for putting up with me while I was preoccupied with this work.

PART I

Understanding financialization

1. Introduction

WHAT IS FINANCIALIZATION?

Profound transformations have taken place both in the US and in the global economy in the last decades. One salient feature of this era has been the dramatic changes that have taken place in the realm of finance. Both the size and importance of financial transactions have been growing continuously. Financial markets and agents have acquired an increasingly prominent position in the economy. The size and profitability of the financial sector have increased. Incomes derived from financial sources as opposed to nonfinancial sources have grown, while total debt in the economy has skyrocketed. The engagement of nonfinancial corporations (NFCs) in financial businesses has increased, as have their investments in financial assets and financial subsidiaries. At the same time, the involvement of financial markets and institutions in the decision-making processes of the NFCs has also increased, leading them to allocate a larger share of their funds to financial markets. In short, '[i]t is difficult to escape the impression that we live in a world of finance' (Krippner 2005: 173).

Various aspects of these transformations, in relation both to domestic economies and to the international financial system, have attracted the attention of economists as well as scholars from other disciplines. Some have labeled all or parts of these transformations as 'financialization.' The concept has been used to designate diverse phenomena, including the globalization of financial markets, the rise of financial investments and incomes derived from these investments, the rise of the 'shareholder value' movement and related changes in corporate governance theories and practices.

Financialization has evolved into a concept similar to 'globalization:' a widely used term without a clear, agreed-upon definition. The precise form and usage of the term have been ambiguous. As a result, there now exist various definitions and uses of the term, as reflected in a recent volume on financialization (Epstein 2005), which brings together a diverse set of articles on various dimensions of financialization. In the introduction, Epstein (2005) acknowledges this situation and chooses to define financialization very broadly as 'the increasing role of financial motives, financial markets, financial actors and financial institutions in the operation of the domestic and international economies' (p. 3). Given the vagueness and ambiguity of

3

the term, I need to define what I mean by financialization for the purposes
of this book. However, before attempting to provide a definition of my
own, there is merit in briefly looking at different definitions used in the literature in order to show the broad and diverse ways in which the concept
of financialization has been used.

For example, Dore (2002), whose focus has been institutional changes in
the last decades, provides a broad definition of the concept, a definition at
least as broad as Epstein's 2005 one:

> the increasing dominance of the finance industry in the sum total of economic
> activity, of financial controllers in the management of corporations, of financial
> assets among total assets, of marketed securities, and particularly of equities,
> among financial assets, of the stock market as a market for corporate control in
> determining corporate strategies, and of fluctuations in the stock market as a
> determinant of business cycles. (pp. 116–17)

The definitions of financialization used in newspaper columns, where the
term has also become fashionable in the last few years, generally display a
similar broadness and elusiveness. For example, Kevin Philips – whose use
of the term in various places popularized it – defines financialization in the
New York Times as follows: 'The process of money movement, securities
management, corporate reorganization, securitization of assets, derivatives
trading and other forms of financial packaging are steadily replacing the
act of making, growing, and transporting things' ('The cycles of financial
scandal,' 17 July 2002).

He adds, in *The Nation*:

> the financialization of America since the 1980s – by which I mean the shift of
> onetime savings deposits into mutual funds, the focus on financial instruments,
> the giantization of the financial industry and the galloping preoccupation of
> corporate CEOs with stock options instead of production lines – has been a
> major force of economic polarization. ('Dynasties!', 8 July 2002)

To cite another example from the popular uses of the concept, British
journalist Eamonn Fingleton labels the same process 'financialism' and
defines it as 'the increasing tendency by the financial sector to invent gra-
tuitous work for itself that does nothing to address society's real needs but
simply creates jobs for financial professionals' (Fingleton 1999, quoted in
Phillips 2006).

Wade (2005) provides a more elaborated definition of financialization
based on three developments:

> Financialization refers to the growing dominance of the financial economy
> over the real economy, as seen in (a) the tightening institutional interlock and

normative congruence around the interests of wealth holders, (b) the rapid redistribution of national income towards capital-owners and away from labor (dependent on wages and salaries), and (c) the rapid redistribution of national income towards the richest 10%, and 1% of households. (Wade 2005: 4)

In Wade's definition, 'institutional interlock' can be seen as the key feature of financialization, as

> other economic institutions – such as corporations, households, and the pension industry – come to organize themselves around financial markets. It has occurred by the stock market becoming the economy's pivotal institution. In the corporate sector institutional interlock with finance comes through the transformation of managers' financial incentives and their perceptions of their responsibilities. Their remuneration increasingly takes the form of stock options rather than salaries; and at senior levels they are recruited from the external labor market rather than promoted from within. Both things together promote the notion that maximization of shareholder value is their sole legitimate objective. They raise or lower budgets, buy or sell bits of companies, with the objective of raising the share prices, not only because they gain directly from stock options but also because the higher share price reduces the chances of hostile take-over – and their ouster. (Wade 2005: 9)

For Duménil and Lévy (2004b), financialization designates the structural change in the post-1980 era characterized by 'the growth of financial enterprises, the rising involvement of nonfinancial enterprises in financial operations, the holding of large portfolios of shares and other securities by households, and so on' (p. 82). Stockhammer (2004), who acknowledges the vagueness of the concept, narrows the definition and uses the concept particularly in relation to the NFCs: 'financialization will be defined as the engagement of nonfinancial businesses in financial markets' (p. 721). Following Arrighi (1994), who is one of the first authors to use the term though without a clear definition, Krippner (2005) employs a relatively narrow definition, too: 'I define financialization as a pattern of accumulation in which profits accrue primarily through financial channels rather than through trade and commodity production' (p. 174).

Not only have the definitions of financialization been numerous and/or unclear, but the composition of the set of works that employ the concept of financialization has also been quite diverse. For example, Randy Martin, a professor of art and public policy, uses the concept in analysing the effects of the increase in the influence of financial calculations and judgments on everyday life in his book *Financialization of Daily Life* (2002).[1]

For the purposes of this study, I use the term at two levels: one broad and another more specific that is better suited for analytical use. At the general level, financialization refers to an increase in the size and significance of financial markets, transactions, and institutions. At a narrower level, I use financialization to designate changes in the relationship between the non-financial corporate sector and financial markets. These latter changes include, first, an increase in financial investments and hence financial incomes of the NFCs; and second, an increase in financial market pressure on the management of NFCs. This increase in pressure, which is revealed through governance debates revolving around 'shareholder value,' results in an increasing transfer of resources from NFCs to financial markets in the forms of interest payments, dividend payments and stock buybacks. While I discuss how to develop an understanding of the financialization process in the first part of this book, I will be using the more general definition; and in the second part, when I analyse the impact of financialization on the nonfinancial corporate sectors' rate of capital accumulation I will be referring to the second and narrower level of this definition. But before then, let me briefly discuss the major questions raised about financialization.

ISSUES AROUND FINANCIALIZATION

In general, financialization is associated with a rise in the share of national income accruing to the holders of financial assets and a concomitant decline in the share of labor, an increase in financial instability, slower growth and dimmer prospects for economic prosperity. Some of the effects of financialization – along with the trends toward globalization and neoliberalism that accompanied it – have been highly detrimental to a significant percentage of people around the globe. Accordingly, finding ways to mitigate the deleterious effects of financialization has been a central concern. Most of the literature, hence, has been concerned with negative effects of financialization, as we will see in the following chapters. However, before moving onto that, outlining the main issues around financialization would be useful to contextualize this book.

As revealed by the discussion of the various definitions of the term financialization, there is indeed quite a wide range of issues addressed in relation to this concept. No matter how the term is defined, however, the first step is to determine a measure of financialization (Krippner 2005; Crotty 2005). As Krippner (2005) notes, before any discussion of financialization and its impacts on the rest of the economy, 'we ought to first determine whether it is in fact accurate to characterize the US economy as having been "financialized"' (p. 174). She then provides a detailed presentation of the financialization of the American economy through a careful study of various macro data sources. Crotty (2005), in a broad discussion of financialization as one of the important components of the global neoliberal regime, documents various aspects of financialization for the US nonfinancial corporate sector, while Duménil and Lévy (2005) undertake a similar endeavor for both the US and France. These works unveil three important phenomena: NFCs have been increasing their financial investments relative to their real investments; they are earning a larger share of their profits from financial operations; and NFCs are discharging higher proportions of their earnings to the financial markets in the forms of interest payments, dividends and stock buybacks.

While documenting financialization has been an important research area, others, at least as important, are the analyses of the origins and underlying dynamics of it. The central question posed in these studies can be stated thus: why did financialization begin around the early 1980s? While mainstream economic theory has been mostly silent as to the origins of financialization, several heterodox scholars, including Arrighi (1994, 2003 and 2005), Arrighi and Silver (1999), Harvey (2003), Sweezy (1997) and Amin (1996, 2003), provide answers to this fundamental question. Arrighi's approach, in particular, has attracted much attention. While most of these analyses locate the origin of financialization in the accumulation crisis faced in the 1970s, there are other contributions arguing that the roots of financialization are to be found in changes in financial markets caused by deregulation and liberalization. Duménil and Lévy (2005) focus on a third set of explanations; they emphasize the role of politics and class dynamics in the financialization process.

The macroeconomic dynamics of financialization in the US economy is a third topic of discussion. In particular, Boyer (2000), Aglietta (2000) and Aglietta and Breton (2001) provide attempts to understand these dynamics. Stockhammer (2004), who confirms some trends associated with financialization, analyses their effects on the capital accumulation of NFCs in the US.

Fourth, the changes that have taken place in corporate governance and their implications for corporate performance constitute a lively terrain of debate. The rise of the 'shareholder value' movement, the alignment of managerial and shareholder interests and their consequences are discussed by many including Lazonick and O'Sullivan (2000), Froud et al. (2000), Feng et al. (2001), Bivens and Weller (2004), Henwood (1997 and 2003), Morin (2000) and Jürgens et al. (2000). Moreover, Soederberg (2003), Singh (2003) and Glen et al. (2000) discuss the implications of the promotion of US style corporate governance in 'developing' countries.

Fifth, the era of financialization has been characterized by rising income inequality and a decline in the conditions of labor. This has attracted interest in explorations of changes in income distribution. Epstein and Jayadev (2005) document the fact that in a large sample of Organisation for Economic Co-operation and Development (OECD) member countries, the share of national income going to 'rentiers' (financial institutions and holders of financial assets) rose in the 1980s and 1990s. Duménil and Lévy (2004c) thoroughly examine the changes in income distribution due to financialization. Lazonick and O'Sullivan (2000) document the effects of financialization on labor through corporate downsizing and higher financial payments.

A distinct but related debate is that of comparing financial systems. The US system in which financial markets are central has been compared with the German-type systems in which banks occupy a central place. Although the term financialization is not used in this debate, comparison between bank-based and market-based financial systems is the focus (for overviews of this debate, see Mayer 1988; Schaberg 1999; Ndikumana 2005).

Last but not least, changes in international financial relations are another topic of discussion. The explosion of international financial transactions, changes in the international monetary system and the burgeoning of financial crises in 'developing countries' are widely discussed (see, for example, Babb 2005; Akyüz and Boratav 2005; O'Connell 2005; Crotty and Lee 2005). Blecker (2005) shows the implications of financialization for international trade and finance theories. Many call attention to the unsustainability of financialization at the international level, while various works discuss international financial crises (see, for example, D'Arista 2005; Grabel 2005; Felix 2005).

OUTLINE OF THE BOOK

I hope to contribute to the literature on financialization in three ways with this book. First, I outline a framework through which we can understand the factors that led to the financialization of the US economy by providing stylized facts on financialization within a historical context and critically reviewing different perspectives on financialization. Second, I analyse the macroeconomic impacts of financialization on the investment behavior of the nonfinancial corporate sector. After developing a theoretical framework that highlights potential negative impacts of financialization on the capital accumulation process, I analyse aggregate US data to test the theoretical hypotheses. Third, using a data set for large US nonfinancial corporations, I analyse the impacts of financialization on firm behavior. This firm level exercise not only helps to overcome the problems associated with aggregate time-series analysis but also allows me to analyse diverse effects of financialization on different types of firms.

The rest of the book is organized as follows. In the first part of the book, composed of Chapters 2, 3 and 4, I outline a framework for understanding financialization. I begin in Chapter 2 with an empirical documentation of the financialization trends of the post-1980 era in comparison with the earlier 'Golden Age' period. Simple time-series descriptions are useful in concretizing the phenomena at the center of the financialization literature. The following chapter provides a historical context to interpret the financial expansion of recent decades. Starting with the 'finance capital' era of the late 19th and early 20th centuries, I discuss the changing role of finance within the economy throughout the 20th century. Chapter 4 provides a critical overview of the financialization literature. While discussing various strengths and weaknesses of the main works in this literature and highlighting the contributions of different perspectives, this chapter aims to improve our understanding of financialization by presenting it as part of a historical and contradictory process and concludes with a general framework to help that.

In the next part of the book, I explore further the relationship between the financial and nonfinancial sectors of the economy. Here I focus on the potential impacts of financialization on the investment behavior of NFCs. Chapter 5 develops a theoretical framework that analyses effects of financialization on capital accumulation. In this chapter, I first discuss the changing flow of funds between financial markets and NFCs and then I seek to explore the effects of increased financialization on the real investment decisions of NFCs. Specifically, I outline two channels that have been developed in the theoretical literature. First, I ask whether increased financial investment and increased financial profit opportunities crowd out real investment by changing the incentives of the NFC managers and directing funds away from real investment. Second, I examine whether increased payments to financial markets impede real investment by decreasing available internal funds, shortening the planning horizon of the NFC management and increasing uncertainty.

Hence, this chapter and the following chapters, which provide empirical support for the theoretical approach developed in this chapter, contribute to the debates around the effects of financialization on the capital accumulation process. There has been much discussion on the relation between financialization and real capital accumulation. For example, Crotty (2005) describes a form of financialization in which NFCs have started to increase their investment in financial assets, bought or expanded financial subsidiaries and shortened their planning horizons. Duménil and Lévy (2004a) draw attention to the fact that interest and dividend payments to financial markets have been on the rise and they argue that NFCs are therefore left with smaller amounts of funds for real investment. Aglietta and Breton (2001) make the same point and argue that an active market for corporate control pushes firms to boost their share prices through dividend payouts or stock buybacks and, as a consequence, the share of earnings devoted to financing growth is reduced. Stockhammer (2004) attempts to empirically trace the link between financialization and capital accumulation at the macroeconomic level and argues that investment in financial assets by NFCs indicates a change in management objectives towards adopting 'rentier preferences.'

Using aggregate data for the US, I provide an analysis of the effects of financialization on real investments of NFCs in Chapter 6. The data suggest that there has been a sharp increase in financial investments undertaken by the nonfinancial sector after 1980, as well as an unambiguous increase in the payments made to the financial sector. I then provide econometric evidence that the increase in financial investments and in financial payments made to financial markets has had negative effects on the aggregate capital accumulation behavior of the nonfinancial corporate sector. In Chapter 7, I seek to empirically explore the relationship between financialization in the US economy and real investment at the firm level. Using data from a sample of NFCs from 1973 to 2003, I find a negative relationship between investment and financialization at the firm level. While this result reinforces the results of the earlier analysis, it also provides insights into across-firm characteristics of financialization.

Finally, in the last chapter, I bring together conclusions of the analyses carried out in the previous chapters and outline further areas of research that would contribute to a complete understanding of financialization and its implications.

NOTE

1. There is even an 'International Working Group on Financialization' in formation which is 'interested in financialization and all the issues around relations between the capital market, firms and households' (see www.iwgf.org).

2. Stylized facts

In the first chapter, I opted for a definition of financialization at two distinct levels. At the most general level, it refers to an increase in the size, profitability and significance of the financial sector. At the NFC level, financialization is defined as the increase in both financial investments and hence financial incomes of NFCs and the increase in the amount of payments to financial markets. Here, I present detailed descriptive statistics that demonstrate these financialization trends of the post-1980 era in the US economy at both levels. These data show a continuous increase in the size and profitability of the financial sector, a secular growth in the volume of financial transactions, as well as financialization of NFCs. Before moving onto a discussion of the historical context of financialization and the theories that attempt to explain this process, it is important to depict what has actually changed in the last decades.

Since the 1980s, world financial markets have been growing rapidly. The value of total global financial assets (equities, government and corporate debt securities and bank deposits) reached to 140 trillion dollars by the end of 2005 from 12 trillion in 1980, 64 trillion in 1995 and 93 trillion in 2000. Stock of global financial assets was 338 percent of the global Gross Domestic Product (GDP) in 2005, up from 109 percent in 1980 (Farrell et al. 2007: 8). For the US economy, the stock of financial assets reached 303 percent of the GDP in 1995 and 405 percent in 2005 (ibid., p. 10).[1] One needs to remember that this definition of financial assets only include the most basic ones and adding all other types of financial assets would only increase these ratios.

A significant indicator of the increasing salience of finance within the economy is the share of national income that goes to the financial sector. As Figure 2.1 demonstrates, total income acquired by the finance, insurance and real estate (FIRE) sector has been increasing since the early 1980s.[2] While in the 1952–1980 period, the share of national income that went to the FIRE sector hovered between 12 and 14 percent, by the 2000s it had approached 20 percent. Behind the rise in this ratio lies an increased profitability of the financial sector. Figure 2.2 shows financial corporations' profits as a percent of NFCs' profits. This ratio shows a significant increase after the mid-1980s, with an explosion in the 1990s. Financial corporations' profitability with respect to NFCs' profitability reached historical heights at

Note: FIRE income in BEA statistics is calculated using SIC for years prior to 1998 and NAICS thereafter. The relative decline in FIRE income ratio after 1998 seems to be due to the switch to NAICS classification.

Source: BEA NIPA Table 6.1.

Figure 2.1   FIRE income as a percent of national income, 1952–2006

the beginning of the 2000s and started to decline thereafter, though it remained above the maximum of all earlier periods. The decline in the ratio in the mid-2000s is due not to a decline in financial corporations' profits but to a strong recovery in NFC profits. A similar trend is observed in the profitability of commercial banks, presented in Figure 2.3.[3] After a significant decline in commercial bank profitability in the late 1980s, these banks started earning record profits in the 1990s.[4]

The growing importance of the financial sector within the economy is also reflected by the increase in the number of people the sector employs and the total compensation provided to these employees. Employment in the financial sector as a percent of total employment has been on the rise since the early 1950s as seen in Figure 2.4. This ratio went from 3 percent in 1952 to more than 5 percent in the late 1980s. After 1990, the ratio of financial sector employment to total employment started declining and hovered between 4 and 5 percent. However, the compensation of financial sector employees continued to increase. Figure 2.5 shows the compensation of financial sector employees as a percent of total compensation. The

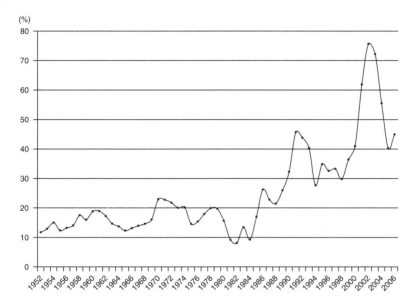

Note: The decline in the ratio in mid-2000s is due not to a decline in financial corporations' profits but to a strong recovery in NFC profitability.

Source: BEA NIPA Table 6.16.

Figure 2.2 Financial corporations' profits as a percent of NFCs' profits, 1952–2006

trends in the two figures are similar while the rise in financial sector employees' compensation is more significant after 1980 and by 2005 this ratio reached almost double the 1952–1980 average. We observe that the financial sector has been using up more resources while receiving an increasing share of the total compensation in the economy.

With the increase in financial sector profitability, employment and compensation levels, we also observe a significant increase in the so-called 'rentier income share,' which is defined as profits from financial market activity of the financial industry (banks, stockbrokers and insurance companies) plus interest income realized by all nonfinancial nongovernment resident units as a share of Gross National Income (Epstein and Jayadev 2005). From 1960 to 1999, this rentier share has more than doubled, as can be seen in Table 2.1.[5]

Increases in the volume of financial transactions in the financialization era are more spectacular. For example, the average daily trading volume in the New York Stock Exchange (NYSE) increased from 3 to 45 million shares between 1960 and 1980. This average, as shown in Figure 2.6,

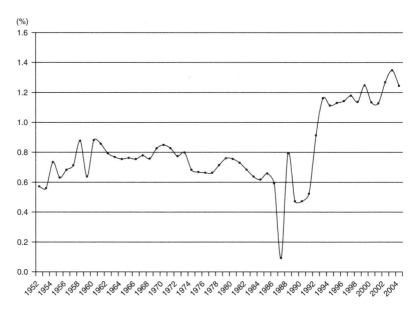

Source: FDIC historical statistics on banking.

*Figure 2.3   Commercial banks' net income as a percent of total assets,
              1952–2004*

reached 200 million shares in the late 1980s, a billion towards the end of
the 1990s and kept increasing throughout the 2000s. A more spectacular
increase was observed in NASDAQ in the 1990s although this changed
with the collapse in the early 2000s. The stock turnover ratio in the NYSE
has also increased dramatically. Figure 2.7 shows that this ratio in the
2000s was five times higher than the average of the 1960s and 1970s. This
latest figure not only indicates increased activity in the stock market, but
also shows that stockholders started holding their stocks for shorter and
shorter time periods, revealing a very short-time horizon for shareholders.
Similar increases have also been observed in the trading of other financial
assets. The average daily trading volume in US Treasury debt securities
increased from 95.7 billion dollars in 1992 to 497.9 billion dollars in 2004
(Grahl and Lysandrou 2006: 957). The daily turnover ratio for US
Treasuries rose to 12 percent in 2004 from an average of 6 percent in 2000
(ibid.).

Another major change in this era took place in the relations between
NFCs and financial markets. On the one hand, NFCs increased their
involvement in financial activities and investment, while on the other hand
they discharged higher proportions of their earnings to financial markets.

Source: BEA NIPA Table 6.5.

Figure 2.4   Financial sector employment as a percent of total employment, 1952–2006

Figure 2.8 depicts the ratio of NFC financial assets to tangible assets and the share of these financial assets within NFCs' total assets. While these ratios stayed almost constant until the early 1980s, after then we observe a tremendous increase in the accumulation of financial assets by NFCs. By the year 2000, NFCs' financial assets equaled tangible assets. This huge rise in NFC financial assets is all the more perplexing given that half of them are classified as 'miscellaneous assets' in the Flow of Funds Accounts, as Figure 2.9 shows. While NFC investment in most other financial asset categories declined, this unidentified portion has been on the rise. This part is likely to include stock market investments of the NFCs as well as accumulated goodwill, although, as Crotty (2005) noted, what is included in this portion of financial assets is a mystery to Federal Reserve economists, too (p. 104).[6]

This increase in financial investments of NFCs is also reflected by the financial income they derive from these investments. Figure 2.10 shows the interest and dividend incomes of NFCs as a percent of their gross value added. Since there is no readily available data on the capital gains NFCs make on the financial assets they hold, this picture does not give a full account of their financial earnings. Still, the increase in this measure

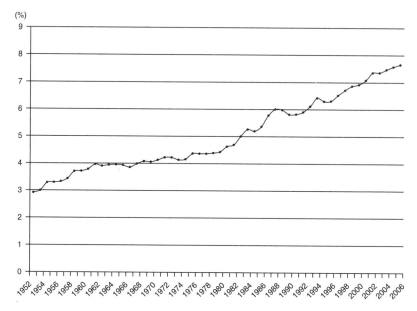

Source: BEA NIPA Table 6.2.

Figure 2.5   *Compensation of financial sector employees as a percent of*
total compensation, 1952–2006

Table 2.1   *Average rentier share in the US as a percentage of GNP*

	1960s	1970s	1980s	1990s
Rentier share average	16.93	24.02	37.45	35.24
Inflation adjusted rentier share average	6.00	3.03	19.61	18.82

Source: Epstein and Jayadev 2005, Tables 3.1 and 3.3.

of NFC financial income is noteworthy.[7] This increase has recently
attracted much attention from the business press as well with the record-
breaking financial profits of the retail firm Sears Holdings Corporation.
According to a *Wall Street Journal* article, Sears 'earned more than half
its net income in the fiscal third quarter ended Oct. 28 from investments
in exotic derivatives designed to mirror the performance of company
stocks' (Covert and McWilliams 2006).[8] This type of financialization of
the NFCs is not limited solely to the US economy. As the April 2006
IMF World Economic Outlook showed, similar trends can be observed in

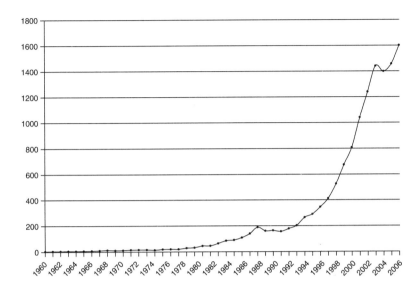

Source: NYSE Factbook Historical Statistics.

Figure 2.6   NYSE average daily volume (million shares), 1960–2006

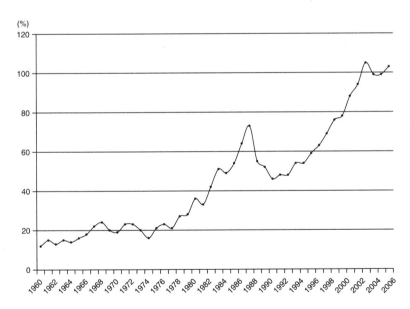

Source: NYSE Factbook Historical Statistics.

Figure 2.7   NYSE stock turnover rate (percent), 1960–2006

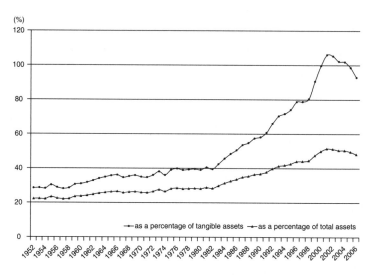

Source: FFA Table B.102.

Figure 2.8   NFC financial assets as a percent of tangible assets and total assets, 1952–2006

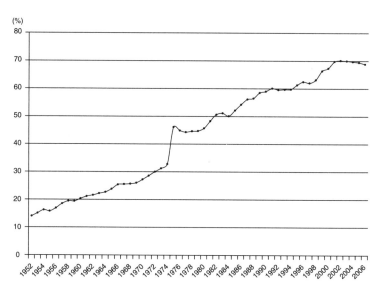

Source: FFA Table B.102.

Figure 2.9   NFCs' miscellaneous financial assets as a percent of total financial assets, 1952–2006

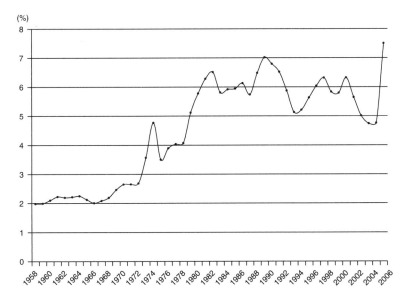

Source: BEA NIPA Tables 1.14, 7.10 and 7.11.

*Figure 2.10   Interest and dividend income of NFCs as a percent of NFC
gross value added, 1958–2006*

countries such as Canada, Germany, the United Kingdom and Japan, especially in the 2000s.[9]

The other side of the financialization of NFCs has been an increase in the financial payments these corporations make. Gross interest payments have been significantly higher in the 1980–2000s period than in the previous era, as can be seen in Figure 2.11. This is not surprising given that real interest rates have been much higher in this period. Figure 2.12 depicts real interest rates, which exhibit the same trend.[10] Although declining interest rates of the early 2000s led to a decline in the NFC interest payments, it is likely that the rising interest rates after 2004 will increase these payments again. At the same time, NFCs increased payments made to shareholders. While dividend payments increased, especially in the 1990s, as shown in Figure 2.13, after the 1980s NFCs also used stock buybacks to distribute earnings to shareholders. Figure 2.14 shows that, with the exception of the early 1990s, the stock market has not been a place to raise capital but rather to discharge earnings.[11]

All these statistics demonstrate that the financial sector has acquired a significantly different and a much larger place in the US during the financialization era. This period has been characterized by rising financial

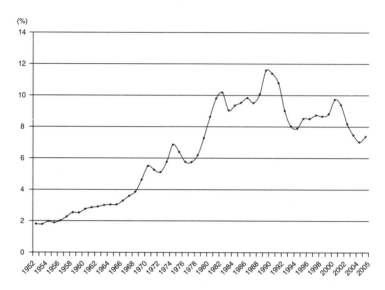

Source: BEA NIPA Tables 1.14 and 7.11.

*Figure 2.11   NFC interest payments as a percent of NFC gross value
added, 1952–2005*

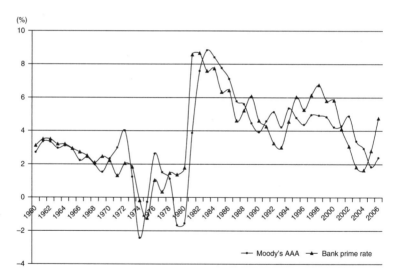

Source: Economic Report of the President Tables B63 and B73.

*Figure 2.12   Moody's AAA bond rate and bank prime rate (adjusted for
inflation), 1960–2006*

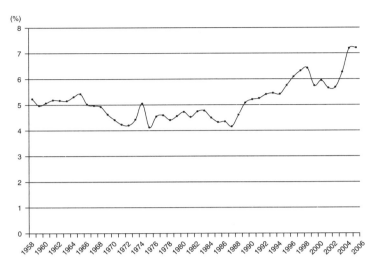

Source: BEA NIPA Tables 1.14 and 7.10.

Figure 2.13 *NFC dividend payments as a percent of NFC gross value added, 1958–2006*

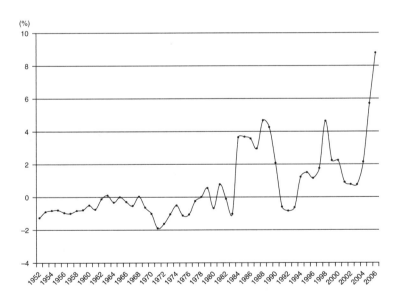

Source: BEA NIPA Table 1.14 and FFA Table F. 102.

Figure 2.14 *NFC stock buybacks as a percent of NFC gross value added, 1952–2006*

profits, the increasing size of the financial sector in all aspects, exploding financial transactions volumes and increasing financialization of NFCs. While these statistics show the extent of the transformations, a look at the historical developments in the financial markets and in their relationship to the rest of the economy would help to contextualize these numbers. The next chapter provides this historical review.

NOTES

1. For detailed statistics on global financial markets and capital flows see the *Third Annual Report of the McKinsey Global Institute* (Farrell et al. 2007).
2. FIRE sector includes 'real estate' which indeed is not part of the financial sector. However, for these statistics, it is not possible to exclude it since the Bureau of Economic Analysis's 'national income by industry' data (National Income and Product Accounts Table 6.1) does not make this distinction. 'Real estate' is not included in any additional presentation of statistics, that is, in the instances where it is possible to get data for the financial sector itself. It should also be noted that statistics are calculated using SIC for years prior to 1998 and NAICS thereafter.
3. Across advanced economies the behavior of financial sector profits in the last two decades differed considerably. While in the US, France and Japan the profits of the financial sector have been rising, they have been falling in Italy and not showing any trend in Germany or the UK (IMF 2006: 144). The IMF (2006) argues that '[t]his cross-country variation may reflect differences in regulatory frameworks and in macroeconomic conditions that have affected both the intensity and the timing with which global patterns have impacted national financial systems' (p. 144).
4. Crotty (2007) notes that this rise in the profitability of the financial sector has not been adequately explained. The deregulation in the financial markets, removal of barriers to accessing other national markets and the technological advances created fierce competition in this era and led to 'the coexistence of historically high profit rates in most financial industries with what appears to be intense competition' (p. 4). He refers to this as 'Volcker's paradox' after the following remark by Paul Volcker:

   > We have reached the magic hour. I had another comment I was going to make. You won't be able to resolve it for me but I'll raise it anyway. It strikes me that when one looks at the banking system, never before in our lifetime has the industry been under so much competitive pressure with declining market share in many areas and a feeling of intense strain, yet at the same time, the industry never has been so profitable with so much apparent strength. How do I reconcile those two observations? (FDIC 1997, p. 118, quoted in Crotty 2007: 5)

   Crotty (2007) argues that there are four over-lapping reasons behind this paradox:

   > First, the demand for financial products and services has grown exponentially. Competition is least corrosive of profitability in periods of strong demand. Second, there has been a rapid rise in concentration in most wholesale and global financial markets as well as in several important domestic retail markets. Three to seven firm concentration ratios are now quite high. This has created an important precondition for what Schumpeter called 'corespective' competition – an industry regime in which large firms compete in many ways, but avoid the kinds of competitive actions such as price wars that significantly undercut industry profit. Third, there is substantial evidence that large financial institutions have raised their profit rates by taking on

greater risk, risk that is partially hidden from view because much of it is located off-balance-sheet. . . . Fourth, giant commercial and investment banks have turned innovation into a core business. They create and trade ever more complex derivative products in ever higher volume. They have been able to achieve high margins on much of this business by selling the bulk of their products over-the-counter (OTC) rather than on exchanges, thus insulating the profit margin from destructive competition. (pp. 5–6)

5. For a comprehensive analysis and estimates of the rentier share in various OECD countries see Power et al. (2003), Epstein and Power (2003), and Epstein and Jayadev (2005).

6. Flow of Funds Accounts classify the following items under 'miscellaneous financial assets:' US Direct Investment Abroad, Insurance Receivables, Equity in federal government-sponsored enterprises (GSEs), Investment in Finance Company Subsidiaries, and other miscellaneous assets. Among these items, 'other miscellaneous assets' occupy the largest portion (see FFA Tables B.102 and F. 102).

7. Krippner (2005) uses data gathered from Internal Revenue Services (IRS) publications, which include capital gains. She shows the same increasing trend of financial incomes, which she calls 'portfolio income,' when capital gains are included.

8. At the macro level, we have little information about the types of financial assets that NFCs invest in. The Sears example is interesting in that it gives an idea on this issue:

> The company turned an investment in derivatives in other companies' shares into a $101 million after-tax profit during the quarter. . . . The financial derivatives used by Sears, known as 'total-return swaps' are agreements that take on the big risks of highly leveraged investments in equities or other assets without actually buying them or assuming debt to purchase them. (Covert and McWilliams 2006)

9. According to this report:

> [s]ince the 1980s, the corporate sector of the G-7 economies has swung from being a large net borrower of funds from other sectors of the economy to a net lender of funds. Indeed, on average over 2002–04, the excess saving (or 'net lending') of the corporate sector – defined as the difference between undistributed profits (gross saving) and capital spending – was at a historic high of 2½ percent of GDP in the G-7 countries. . . . This behavior has been widespread, taking place in economies that have experienced strong economic growth (Canada, the United Kingdom, and the United States) and in those where growth has been relatively weak (Europe and, until recently, Japan). (IMF 2006: 136)

10. Real interest rates in these figures are simply calculated by subtracting the rate of inflation from nominal interest rates.

11. Crotty (2005) documents a similar trend by looking at the share of total financial payments (interest payments, dividends and stock buybacks) within NFC cash flow. This ratio exceeds 70 percent at the end of the 1990s (see pp. 96–9).

3. Historical context

FINANCE CAPITAL AT THE TURN OF THE 19TH CENTURY

The prominence of finance in the post-1980 world raises the question of similarities with the period of late 19th to early 20th century, as in this period too, finance was seen as the dominant force in the economy. Comparisons across eras may not be of too much use as there are too many factors to account for change and capitalism cannot necessarily be characterized by compartmentalized sub-epochs. However, these historical comparisons can still be useful in understanding the current forms of capital accumulation and institutional configurations. In this context, we can unravel the role of finance at different points in time and gain a better understanding of the continuous adjustments and restructurings in the system. When we look at the US economy at the turn of the 19th century, we see a period that was characterized by a large and powerful financial sector accompanied by a monopolization/oligopolization process in the economy. NFCs in the US were said to be under the influence (or under the control) of the Money Trust – an association of financial firms under the leadership of J.P. Morgan's bank.[1] This was the result of investment bankers responding to the cutthroat competition of the 1880s and 1890s by turning their attention to the financing of cartels, trusts and mergers (Heilbroner and Singer 1984: 208).[2] For example, in 1904 a single firm or two firms that were put together by a merger controlled more than half of the output in 78 different industries (ibid.).

This period is described by historians as one in which competition was kept in limits through what Chernow (1990) calls a 'gentleman banker's code,' which essentially meant that the Money Trust acted coherently to resolve many of the problems and conflicts in the core industries of the period, especially the destructive competition which created and reproduced large excess capacity that led to cutthroat pricing and low profits. These financial firms attained their power through loans to large NFCs, buying large amounts of stock and placing representatives on the boards of these corporations. This was a situation resembling Hilferding's ([1910] 1985) account of German bank control of NFC cartels in the early 19th century. Hilferding described a situation in which Germany's *Großbanken* – the largest banks including those of Deutsche, Dresdner and Darmstäder – exercised power over industry. This power was possible, first, by the rise of the 'joint stock company,' which enabled banks to acquire controlling shareholdings; second, by personal linkages through appointment of bank directors onto the boards of industrial corporations; and third, by the knowledge acquired by the banks in their handling of the industrial corporations' finances. According to Hilferding, the fusion of financial and industrial capital was characterized by banks being the dominant partners and imposing change on the industrial corporations. This dominance reached such a level that Hilferding pointed out that social ownership of the industry could be achieved by one simple move of nationalizing this handful of banks.

While Hilferding's account was mostly based on his study of the prevailing system in Germany, in the US, we see that the House of Morgan played a significant role in the economy. For example, in 1895, it would save the gold system and the US government by organizing a rescue fund to reverse the gold outflow from New York and act as a central bank in the financial panic of 1907 (Markham 2002). Large-scale financing needs of the industrial firms in this era contributed to the powerful position of the financial sector. With the American victory in the Spanish-American War, the attention of large NFCs shifted from domestic expansion to a global quest for markets. This new orientation was accompanied by the shifting attention of Wall Street from railroads to industrial trusts. Before the Money Trust took control, key industries suffered from destructive competition. The economies of scale and scope that these industrial trusts made possible could only be sustained in a self-regulatory oligopoly in the absence of any other type of regulation. These industrial trusts achieved a significant degree of vertical integration. For example, the US Steel Trust, of which Carnegie and Morgan were the nucleus, would handle all phases of the business from mining to marketing, hence benefiting from vertical integration.

Late 19th century railroads showed the damage of cutthroat competition 'by causing rate wars among competing companies, a build up of blackmail lines, and lack of standardized gauges' (Chernow 1990: 54).[3] This competition was brought under control by the financiers who offered them the following deal: 'if they refrained from rate-cutting and cutthroat competition, the financiers would stop underwriting competing railways' (ibid., p. 57). In this way, financiers led by the House of Morgan brought order to the railroad industry, which at that point comprised 60 percent of all stock issues on the NYSE. Soon after, the steel industry was subjected to a similar regulation when fear of a railroad-era chaos with its overcapacity and price wars came to dominate. Morgan and his partners came up with a proposal for a trust that would control more than half of the steel business:

> The steel trust was to be a superior sort of conspiracy. Through economies of scale, it would attempt to lower prices and compete in burgeoning world markets. It was a form of national industrial policy, albeit conducted by businessmen for private gain. (ibid., p. 83)

In 1902, the formation of a shipping trust served a similar function by providing cooperation among competitors in the industry where there were too many ships and destructive rate wars. Hence finance assumed a regulatory role in which 'America's most famous financier was a sworn foe of free markets' (ibid., p. 54). Indeed, in terms of assessment of investment projects and allocation of funds, De Long (1991) argues that Morgan's actions resembled to a centralized investment planning directorate.

The significant power and domination of finance capital over industry, personified in the House of Morgan rapidly expanded because American industry was in its infant stage, with opportunities to expand. Since many firms simply did not have the retained earnings to meet their financing requirements, they had to rely on Wall Street bankers who seem to have accumulated their wealth through colonial trade.[4] (As an exceptional case, Rockefeller financed the Standard Oil Trust out of cash reserves accumulated in Standard Oil.) Towards the end of the century, industrial securities started to dominate the financial markets, exceeding the size of railroads and government borrowing (De Long 1991). Hence, in addition to bringing order to the nonfinancial sector where chaos had ruled, the financial sector also fulfilled the financing needs of an expanding industry. Especially when a corporation needed to raise large funds, more than 10 million dollars in capital, it had to do it through J.P. Morgan & Co. or one of its smaller peers, which were not too many in number:

> In the years before World War I, a corporate security flotation worth more than $10 million invariably passed through one of a very few investment banks – J.P. Morgan and Company; Kuhn, Loeb, and Company; the First National Bank; the National City Bank; Kiddler, Peabody, and Company; and Lee, Higginson, and Company. The partners and directors of these institutions were directors, voting trustees, or major stockholders of corporations with a total capitalization – debt plus equity – including subsidiaries, of nearly $30 billion. . . . In perspective, this sum bore the same relation to the size of the US economy then that $7.5 trillion bears today: it amounted to one and a half years' national product and 40 percent of the country's produced capital. (De Long 1991: 206)

There certainly was an increase in funding requirements of industrial firms as the technological developments in the late 19th century paved the way for larger enterprises to replace smaller units of production. These developments required not only access to increased funding, but also a change in the methods of management. While the industrial trusts and the emerging wave of incorporation created a new institutional framework which had the large corporation backed by finance at its center, the second aspect of this era was the occurrence of what was to be called the 'managerial revolution' (Chandler 1977). The emergence of large corporations was accompanied by a separation between the ownership of the corporation and its management. Managerial personnel took the job of running the corporation. De Long (1991) argues that, both for the United States and Germany:

> the existence of 'finance capitalist' institutions played a significant role in the expansion of managerial capitalism. Investment banker willingness to choose and monitor managers appears to have aided founding families that were attempting to withdraw from active management of their businesses and to diversify their holdings. . . . It is possible to speculate that turn-of-the-century finance capitalists played an important role in catalyzing the development of the managerial hierarchies whose importance is stressed by Chandler. (p. 129)

Hence this period witnessed the rise of managers and increased separation between ownership and management under the increasing dominance of financiers. Pineault (2001) points out that the separation of ownership and management can be seen as a first step in 'financialization' since after the separation the owner is not:

> directly a proprietor of productive capital, his relationship to productive capital is 'financialized' in the sense that productive capital appears as commodified financial capital and the revenue generated by corporate productive capital appears to the capitalists, qua rentier, as a stream of financial payments. (p. 35)

In addition, towards the end of the 19th century, in the case of Rockefeller, we observe the involvement of a giant NFC in financial businesses, a phenomenon that is to be widely observed among NFCs at the end of the next century. As noted previously, John D. Rockefeller financed the Standard Oil Trust out of cash reserves to stay independent of Wall Street. Later on, the profits generated by Standard Oil grew so large that Rockefeller searched for a financial repository and ended up choosing the National City Bank. The amount of funds pumped into the bank was great enough for the industrial empire of Rockefeller to tighten its grasp on banking (Chernow 1990).

The growth of the Money Trust and the industrial trusts were mutually reinforcing in this period. While the Money Trust was quite effective in the creation of industrial trusts, the Money Trust itself was strengthened by the growth of these trusts. An institutional characteristic of banks at that time allowed them to swap shares and board members, without having to formally merge. They were structured as private partnerships, rather than publicly traded companies. Therefore, in this age we do not observe a 'shareholder capitalism' resembling the current financialization era. Dominant financial institutions were not bounded in their practices by the requirement of public disclosure and they related to one another through 'gentlemanly rules of conduct,' rules that made possible the collusive behavior that eliminated cut-throat competition that was deemed wasteful. Of course, the investment banks made huge profits thanks to their position. For example, De Long (1991) estimates that the commissions the bankers received from the creation of US Steel in 1910 was equivalent to a sum as large as 15 billion dollars in today's terms.

In short, the Money Trust provided the necessary conditions for the growth of the giant industrial firms of the era and used its power to reduce cutthroat competition and coherently organize key industries. This feature of finance would stand in contrast to the post-1980 rise of finance, as will be discussed below. However, the dominant role of finance came to an end with the Great Depression and subsequent financial regulations.

FINANCE UNDER REGULATION: FROM GREAT DEPRESSION TO 'GOLDEN AGE'

In the 19th century the task of stabilizing financial markets and institutions in the US economy was left to private institutions and markets. This amounted to leaving the stability in the hands of the upper fraction of the financial system (Duménil and Lévy 2003: 8). Large banks, mostly in New York, were acting as reserve banks until the creation of the Federal Reserve in 1913. However, even after this, control of speculative loans remained as a major problem. The ineffectiveness of the Fed in discouraging these specu-lative bank loans would soon contribute to the stock market crash of 1929 (Dymski 1991). The 1920s were characterized by deregulated markets and a large amount of speculative activity. According to Dymski (1991), over-competition for deposits in the banking sector caused an increase in inter-est costs. This increase led banks to search for high-return loans that ended up being high-risk loans. These speculative loans turned into bad loans, thus contributing to waves of bank defaults and runs. The slide in the stock market that started in the summer of 1929 resulted in 'black Thursday,' 24 October, when millions of shares were dumped at whatever price could be obtained – about 20 million shares were sold that day on the NYSE (Markham 2002: 154). Following the stock market crash of 1929, there were revelations of misconduct on Wall Street and almost 10 000 banks failed. Bank failures were accompanied by 'bank holidays' in various states and eventually the government closed all banks during 6–13 March 1933 (Dymski 1991).

The US financial system was heavily regulated following the Great Depression of the 1930s as a result of the widespread belief that finance was the main culprit behind that depression.[5] The new regulations had two major aims: to ensure the stability of the financial sector and to support the growth and capital accumulation agenda of the era. This regulatory framework was a response to the devastation of the real economy with the crash of speculative financial markets. The 'Keynesian accumulation agenda' called for finance to be a reliable input into the production and investment process, providing credit to NFCs at low cost. Commercial banks were to provide short-term finance while investment banks met long-term financing needs. Finance would serve the needs of productive capital as the labor peace achieved by the 'New Deal' required. Isenberg (2000) points out that the 'possibility of a capital–labor accord rested on the construction of a financial sector that would not be disruptive and would promote growth by financing industrial production' (p. 248). D'Arista (1994a), Dickens (1998), Epstein (1994) and Goodhart (1989), among others, show that there was a supportive framework put in place by the regulations that brought together the Federal Reserve, large banks and large industrial capitalists.[6]

The regulatory framework of this era was constructed through a series of laws including the Banking Acts of 1933 and 1935, the Security and Exchange Act of 1934 and various versions of the Federal Reserve Act. The financial structure of the 'Golden Age' was based on the following features. First, the Federal Deposit Insurance Corporation (FDIC) was created to implement deposit insurance for demand and time deposits in an attempt to avoid bank runs.[7] Second, 'firewalls' were inserted between capital markets and depository institutions. These firewalls, as manifested in the Glass–Steagall Act of 1933, helped to isolate the riskier activities of capital markets from the creators, holders and disseminators of the money supply. Deposit banks were prohibited from underwriting and placing corporate stocks and bonds. The intermediary function of dealing with shares and bonds was reserved solely for investment banks. Moreover, commercial banks were restricted from holding securities labeled speculative, such as company stocks. Third, Regulation Q put limits on deposit interest rates in an attempt to limit excessive competition between banks and provide for reduced loan rates. Finally, each particular type of financial institution was covered by a number of regulations (Isenberg 2000: 249). The FDIC and the Comptroller of the Currency were given increased powers to ensure the prudence of the banking sector and limit competition in and entry to the sector. Stock and/or bond issuing entities were required to make their financial situation public.[8]

Hence, the Golden Age of the US economy after World War II was characterized by a significant degree of financial regulation. Furthermore, this era witnessed oligopolistic markets together with weak foreign competition and a comprehensive macroeconomic management of the economy by the government. Regulation and market segmentation drastically reduced the degree of competition in financial markets in order to avoid a recurrence of the 1929–33 collapse. All these provided a business environment in which the managers of industrial corporations acquired a significant degree of autonomy from both banker and stockholder pressure.

FINANCIAL LIBERALIZATION AND DEREGULATION

By the early 1970s the Golden Age structure had begun to break down in the US. This coincided with the demise of the Bretton Woods framework of international financial regulation based on fixed exchange rates and a dollar standard tied to the gold. The breakdown of the accord among labor, finance and industry in the US was manifested in 'wildcat strikes, accelerating inflation and the numerous financial problems that struck in the 1960s and 1970s' (Isenberg 2000: 265). Significant changes in the financial sector accompanied the accumulating troubles in the rest of the economy. The 1970s witnessed a tendency towards liberalizing finance, accompanied by financial innovations aimed at circumventing financial regulations as well as responding to adverse macroeconomic conditions.

Two questions need to be answered in this regard. First, what were the forces behind finance's drive towards deregulation? And second, why did the regulators and NFCs who were to benefit from the financial regulations permit this? In an attempt to answer these questions I discuss below a host of events in the 1960s and 1970s that paved the way for financial liberalization, including accelerating inflation, the domestic financial problems of the 1960s, the internationalization of production, an increase in the political power of finance and a series of financial innovations. These changes took place in an era of general macroeconomic demise.

Accelerating inflation
The financial structure of the Golden Age was viable on the condition that inflation was kept under control. Banks could tolerate low interest rates and they could finance long-term loans with short-term deposits without a high risk of mismatch as long as inflation stayed in check. However, in the 1970s the rise of inflation pushed this system to its limits. Leaving aside the factors behind this rise,[9] inflation certainly had a dominant influence on the economy in general and financial markets in particular (see D'Arista 1994b: 93–5). As Figure 3.1 shows, the rate of inflation rose during the late

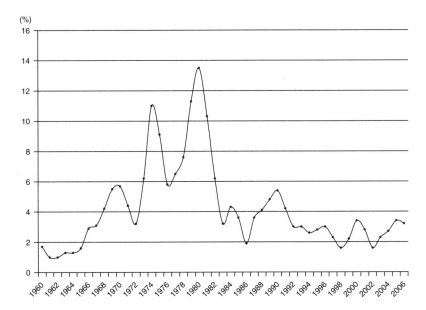

(%)

Note: The inflation rate is calculated using the Consumer Price Index.

Source: Economic Report of the President Table B63.

Figure 3.1   Rate of inflation, 1960–2006

1960s and reached significant heights in the 1970s, before breaking a record after the monetary contraction of the early 1980s. This rise pushed real interest rates down especially after 1973 (as shown above in Figure 2.12) and lowered the profitability of commercial banks (Figure 2.3 above). While lower real interest rates were potentially beneficial to NFCs, reduced financial sector profitability led the sector to search for ways to get around this problem, be it through financial innovations or through forcing deregulation.

Financial troubles of the 1960s
The financial structure of the Golden Age had its first problems in the late 1960s (Isenberg 2000: 253). In order to get the rising inflation under control, the Federal Reserve started to tighten monetary policy, resulting in a credit crunch. Monetary tightening combined with the fiscal effects of the Vietnam War resulted in a rise in nominal interest rates in the 1960s, which led to large corporate borrowers turning towards the small commercial paper market (short-term money market securities issued by private firms) exacerbating commercial banks' problems and expanding the commercial paper market.[10]

Financial innovations

Banks responded with a series of innovations including negotiable certificates of deposit (Coleman 1996: 151). These innovations were designed to retain market share for commercial banks while working around regulations (Coleman 1996: 149). Innovations helped in the push for the dismantling of the regulatory framework by evading the existing regulations and also expanding the financial sector in general. Progress in information and communication technologies supported these financial innovations. As Holmstorm and Kaplan (2001) suggest, together with financial deregulation, these new technologies contributed to the increased dominance of capital markets and later to the rise of the shareholder value movement (p. 2).[11]

One of the financial innovations that used a loophole in the regulations was the entry of non-bank institutions into banking operations. This was part of the process of increased involvement of NFCs in financial businesses. Auto companies already had financial subsidiaries, General Motors Acceptance Corporation (GMAC) and Ford Credit Company (FCC) being the prime examples. GMAC was created in 1919 to provide financing to GM dealers and expanded significantly after World War II. It remained focused on providing auto credits in this era. FCC was founded in 1959 and has grown continuously since then. Toward the end of the 1970s, innovations led to so-called 'hybrid' financial institutions which were tolerated by the regulatory authorities. For example, unlike traditional banks, emerging money-market mutual funds took deposits but did not make loans. On the other side, for example, mortgage companies would make loans but not accept deposits. Some NFCs created affiliated financial companies by taking advantage of this environment. As Kuttner (1997) observes:

> some companies, like Sears and Roebuck, succeeded in breaching not only the wall between commercial banking and investment banking, but the more fundamental wall between finance and commerce, by having affiliated banks, stock brokerages, insurance companies, and real-estate subsidiaries, as well as department stores. (p. 171)

Hence, we can observe the beginnings of the financialization of the nonfinancial corporate sector in this era. Moreover, the development of the commercial paper markets contributed to this movement by allowing NFCs to introduce financing operations:

> The market in commercial paper eliminates the bank's traditional role as judge of credit-worthiness and as middleman. It has removed a reliable and nearly risk-free source of the bank's business. By the same token, most consumers no longer use banks for auto loans, because the auto companies have their own financing operations, selling bonds in the money markets and using the proceeds

to finance loans, sometimes at cut rates in order to promote sales. In some years, Ford Motor Company's profits from its financial business have exceeded its profits from making cars. (Kuttner 1997: 172)

Changes in the needs of industrial capital (internationalization of production)

By the 1970s, a movement towards the internationalization of production was well underway. At the end of the 1960s, a wave of US mergers was accompanied or followed by a move overseas of these merged corporations. As a result, they increasingly gained a multinational character. Constrained by the Glass–Steagall Act, commercial banks were not involved in the financing of the merger wave, but when the large conglomerates that came out of this wave went abroad in search of markets, US commercial banks started to move out in order to meet these corporations' short- and long-term finance needs (Isenberg 2000: 261). Since US banks were constrained by the 'Interest Equalization Tax' which aimed to stop the movement of US dollars abroad, they opened foreign branches to meet the borrowing needs of these multinational corporations.[12] The financing needs arising from internationalization of production is summarized well by J. Ablely, then the chief financial officer of R.J. Reynolds, as '[h]aving banks that are structured to operate around the world in much the same way this company does is crucial' (quoted in Isenberg 2000: 261).[13]

While industrial firms reached their national limits and intensified their pursuit of opening to cross-border operations, the predominant business and economic theories of the era began to claim that regulations and restrictions were barriers to development, employment, profitability and survival. Hence, the success of industrial and productive firms created a powerful push to get rid of the regulatory restrictions to spread to new markets, areas and lines of business. Restrictions on commercial banks and financial intermediaries allowed firms to outgrow their financiers, which contributed to the emergence of an environment in which large NFCs widely supported deregulation to allow financial firms to properly service their growing needs. In other words, as these firms grew, there grew a real demand for larger, more diversified and unrestricted financial services and products. In many ways, the financial sector was at the forefront of demanding deregulation and liberalization but the nonfinancial corporate sector stood to benefit from these changes as well if it created cheaper and easier funding opportunities and helped profitability recover.

The rise of financial power

Another important feature of this era has been the rising power of the financial institutions following the oil shocks of the 1970s. The oil price

hike placed vast amounts of funds in the hands of the oil producing countries. These countries started to recycle their 'petrodollars' through large
New York and European investment banks (Gowan 1999: 20). These banks
suddenly acquired command of massive amounts of funds for which they
started searching for profitable investment opportunities. While they pressured for the opening up of international investment opportunities as the
rates of return in the US and Europe were not good in the slow growth
years of the 1970s, they also acquired a significant amount of influence
through the command of these funds (Gowan 1999; Harvey 2005).
Inadequate demand for these funds prompted the banks to engage in the
process of 'loan pushing.' As a result of this, by 1987, the 15 most heavily
indebted countries owed 402 billion dollars, or about 47.5 percent of their
GDP. In 1982, nine major US commercial banks had advanced loans to
these countries that constituted 288 percent of their bank capital (Russell
2005: 210). The need for international financial opening required by these
banks and their increased power contributed to the pressures towards
financial liberalization and deregulation. The key event was the Mexican
default in 1982, which threatened the solvency of most New York banks.
The 'Washington Consensus' and the pressure on Latin America to liberalize its financial system came as a response to this.

Moreover, the power of the financial sector continued to rise in the post-
1980 era, especially in the 1990s, as debt burgeoned in the US economy. As
Medoff and Harless (1996) contend:

> [i]t is inevitable that lenders become more important in a society where debt
> becomes more important. Therefore, it seems likely that lenders also become
> more powerful. When lenders become more powerful, they have more influence
> over policy; and the policies chosen naturally reflect that influence. (quoted in
> Phillips 2006: 282)

Rise of institutional investors

One of the most significant outcomes of the changes in financial markets
has been the growth of institutional investors.[14] At the beginning of the
1980s, the share of institutional investors' asset holdings in total financial
assets was still much smaller. Figure 3.2 shows that from 1970 to 2002
the share of institutional investors in stock holdings almost doubled.
Investment funds attracted the savings that were previously held in fixed-
term bank deposits. The introduction of funded pension schemes created a
huge rise in the inflow of money into the securities market to buy corporate stocks as well as corporate and government bonds. As Toporowski
(2000) points out, 'when funded pension schemes were being advocated
during the 1970s, one of their supposed main advantages was that they
would provide long-term finance for business expansion' (p. 50).[15] Taxation

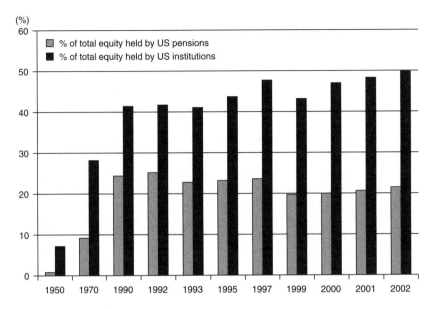

Source: NYSE Factbook Historical Statistics.

Figure 3.2   *Percent of corporate stocks held by institutional investors,
1950–2002*

on finance capital was also reduced, especially on the new pension and investment funds so as to increase the participation of small investors.

While institutional investors gained from the deregulation of securities market commissions, technological advances helped institutional investors increase the efficiency of their trading, clearing and settlement systems and hence drive their costs down. These investors heavily utilized new financial instruments, including mortgage-backed securities and collateralized mortgage obligations which utilized technological advances as they required vast data-processing capabilities (Davis and Steil 2001: 39).

However, the growth in the equity holdings of institutional investors was not uniform across different types. The relative importance of the holdings of mutual funds and pension funds increased in particular (Downes et al. 1999: 1). At the same time, the increased institutional investment contributed to the growth of capital markets and led to increased takeovers, junk bonds and leveraged buyouts (Holmstrom and Kaplan 2001: 2).[16]

Perhaps one of the most important outcomes of the rise in the number of institutional shareholders was the shift in the balance of power from corporate stakeholders to shareholders (Donaldson 1994). That is, the role of institutional investors was not limited to just providing finance for the corporations, they also started to play a significant role in terms of the relationship between managers and shareholders. The rise of institutional investors was one of the most significant dimensions of the transformations in financial markets and had significant impacts on corporate governance changes.

CORPORATE GOVERNANCE CHANGES

In general, corporate governance refers to the relations among various actors in publicly traded corporations and focuses on the rights and obligations of managers and directors in relation to shareholders. Corporate governance mechanisms and practices have changed significantly since the early 1980s. While industrial corporations mostly adopted a strategy of retaining and reinvesting earnings until the 1970s, since then corporate strategy focused on downsizing the corporate labor force and prioritizing the distribution of earnings to shareholders as reflected by the rise in NFC financial payments figures presented above. In this context, management is obliged to satisfy the short-term profit maximization goals of shareholders. This focus was clearly shown in Figure 2.7 above, which depicts the rapid rise of the stock turnover rate. The average shareholder now holds shares for less than a year.

There are three interrelated developments behind the transformations in the corporate governance paradigm. First, the hostile takeover movement of the 1980s created a 'market for corporate control' through which corporations, especially the ones with low financial performances, were subject to takeovers. Second, creating 'shareholder value' became a prominent objective for management and the interests of managers and shareholders were 'aligned' through the introduction of large stock options in the 1990s. Those corporations that do not pay 'adequate' dividends or have low-priced shares in the short run are seen as creating inadequate shareholder value and thus are vulnerable to attack. Third, the emergence and development of 'agency theories' provided the 'theoretical basis' for these transformations. While I discuss these theories in the next chapter, a brief look at the takeover movement and stock options is in order.

Takeover movement
The first step in changing corporate governance has been the creation of a market for corporate control through the takeover movement of the 1980s. This movement was distinguished by the role of hostile bids[17] and the use of leverage. The leveraged buyouts resulted in debt levels typically exceeding

80 percent of total capital (Holmstrom and Kaplan 2001: 1). In this era, nearly half of the major corporations in the US received a takeover offer (Mitchell and Mulherin 1996). What is important in this context is not so much the actual number of takeovers or takeover offers, but rather that all the firms felt the threat of takeover: 'many firms that were not taken over restructured to hostile pressure to make themselves less attractive targets' (Holmstrom and Kaplan 2001: 1) and 'even those firms that were not actually taken over often decided to restructure in response to hostile pressure, particularly when corporate raiders had purchased large blocks of shares' (ibid.: 6). The responses included stock buybacks and special dividends, usually financed by debt.

The origins of the 'market for corporate control' are traced back to the moment when Michael Milken, who was an employee at the investment bank Drexel, Burnham and Lambert, managed to provide a liquid secondary market for junk bonds.[18] In the 1970s, when financial institutions started trading in junk bonds, it was mostly mutual funds – then facing an adverse stock market – that were engaged in this trading. Following financial deregulation, pension funds and insurance companies came to the market as well, soon to be followed by the savings and loan institutions. The entrance of institutional investors to the market as big players has contributed to the creation of a market for corporate control. In the beginning, the main supply of junk bonds came from bonds that were once investment grade bonds but had been downgraded, as well as low grade bonds remaining after the conglomeration mania of the 1960s (Bruck 1988, see also Perry and Taggart 1988; Gaughan 1996). In the early 1980s and especially after the savings and loan institutions entered the market following the Garn–St. Germain Act, junk bonds began to be used to launch hostile takeovers, even against the largest corporations. Hence this wave of takeovers heralded the establishment of a market for corporate control. Theories regarding the market for corporate control were already being developed – as I discuss below – to argue that takeovers were beneficial to the corporations as well as to the economy as a whole. By the early 1980s an effective market for takeovers and corporate control had been established (Lowenstein 2004). Following the formation of this market, corporate management started to focus on distributing their corporate incomes in ways that would support or increase the price of corporate equities.

One significant result of the takeover movement and the creation of a market for corporate control was that it brought management jobs in the corporation under threat:

Takeovers had a similarly energizing effect on managers, in particular on CEOs. Previously, theirs had been the safest jobs around; now, their fortress was under

siege and their pulse rate was on the rise. Given the dreadful state of their companies, a little anxiety was no bad thing. To escape a buyout, CEOs felt they *had*
to raise their share price. This was a significant departure. Previously, stock
prices had been seen as a long-term barometer. Prices in the short term were
notoriously unreliable (this was the lesson of the Great Crash). But with a Henry
Kravis lurking, the long term might not exist. (Lowenstein 2004: 6)

Or, as Gillan argues, from a more mainstream point of view, 'as managers
compete in the product market, assets (companies) go to the highest value
use and thus inefficient managers are disciplined' (2006: 391).

It should also be noted that hostile takeovers were encouraged by tax
regulations. The debt with which the takeovers were financed was tax
deductible and the raider could at the same time take advantage of depre-
ciation write-offs (Kuttner 1997: 180). Furthermore, there were large profits
to be made out of these transactions by the middlemen – institutional
investment managers, investment bankers and lawyers – who happened to
have considerable political influence and hence provided a force for the continuation of the movement (ibid.).

Even though the hostile takeover activity declined after 1987, the pressure on corporations remained acute through the following decade since
the 'hostile pressure from investors with large blocks of shares' (Holmstrom
and Kaplan 2001: 6) remained in place.

Stock options
Faced with the development of a market for corporate control and an
increase in the demands of brokers and fund managers, corporate managers fought back during the 1980s (Useem 1996, esp. Chapter 2). In order
to avoid losing their jobs, they adopted measures including poison pills,
golden parachutes, staggered board terms and so on (ibid.). Moreover,
debt-financed stock buybacks and special dividends were also used.
However, by the 1990s the 'stick' was not the only option used by the
financial markets. Stock options started playing the role of 'carrot' by providing managers with an incentive to increase stock prices. When a
company's stock price increased, managers were able to cash in their stock
options; hence the interests of managers and shareholders were 'aligned.'
As Gillan summarizes: 'during the 1990s academics and practitioners alike
argued in favor of equity-based compensation (particularly stock options)
as a mechanism for aligning the incentives of managers and shareholders'
(2006: 387).

Stock options were not a new invention though. Top managers in many
firms started receiving stock options in the 1950s after tax changes that
made this type of remuneration attractive (Lazonick and O'Sullivan 2000:
24). While stock options became important components of managerial pay

in the 1960s, the downturn in the stock market in the 1970s made them less attractive. However, the 1980s and 1990s witnessed an explosion in stock-based rewards to management. The alignment of shareholder interests with those of management through the vehicle of stock options grants was thus not completely new.

To sum up, significant transformations took place in the financial sector at the end of the 1970s. These transformations coupled with the developments in other parts of the economy gave rise to an era in which finance acquired prominence once again. Rising inflation in the 1970s caused troubles for US financial institutions in their efforts to generate adequate returns and this in turn created a powerful drive for financial deregulation of the American economy. The formation of a liquid market in junk bonds and the emergence of a powerful market for corporate control became significant features of this era. These changes in financial markets produced three significant forces accelerating the rise of financialization. They allowed a general rise in the size, power and profitability of finance; generated opportunities for NFCs to branch into financial activities; and produced the changes in corporate governance practices leading to a rise in the power of financiers and a shortening of NFC planning horizons. In the next chapter, I turn to a review of different perspectives on these transformations, increasingly labeled as financialization.

NOTES

1. Money Trust was the code for Morgan, which held 72 directorships in 112 corporations and controlled the industries of finance, insurance, railroads, transportation and utilities through direct trusts or 'voting trusts' (Chernow 1990).
2. Destructive or cutthroat competition refers to 'situations when competition results in prices that do not chronically or for extended periods of time cover costs of production, particularly fixed costs. This may arise in secularly declining or 'sick' industries with high levels of excess capacity or where frequent cyclical or random demand downturns are experienced' (Khemani and Shapiro 1993). See Crotty (2000) for a review of theories of oligopoly and their role in preventing cutthroat competition and providing co-respective competition.
3. See D'Eramo (2003: 17–22) for a vivid description of destructive and irrational competition in the railroad industry in the 19th century and the following intervention of financiers.
4. According to finance historians, J.P. Morgan & Co. also had a comparative advantage in getting funds from London and Paris, the largest providers of long-term credit at the time (Ramirez 1995).
5. 'In every generation concern has arisen, sometimes to the boiling point. Fear has emerged that the United States might one day discover that a relatively small group of individuals, especially through banking institutions they headed might become virtual masters of the economic destiny of the United States' (Adolf Berle, February 1969, quoted in Markham 2002: vii). Also, see De Long (1991) for a brief review of the political hostility directed towards finance in general and J.P. Morgan in particular.

6. See Isenberg (2000: 248–52) for a succinct overview of the reconstruction of financial markets after the Great Depression.
7. See Dymski (1991) for a detailed examination of the regulation of US banking system in this era.
8. See Khoury (1990) for an overview of the financial regulations of the era.
9. It has been suggested that the decline in the share of total corporate income going to profits led to increased pressures on corporations to raise prices in order to boost profits and to an intensification of the struggle between corporations and employees over the division of that income (see Wolfson 1994: 232 and Rosenberg and Weisskopf 1981). This was exacerbated by the oil price shocks of the 1970s.
10. Commercial papers are a form of uncollateralized short-term debt. They are a substitute for short-term borrowings from commercial banks.
11. For a comprehensive review of financial innovations in this era see Allen and Gale (1994): Chapter 2.
12. Jones (2005) tracks the emergence of multinational corporations and the change in their financing needs in the pre-1980 era.
13. See Moffitt (1983, Chapter 2) for an overview of the effects of the internationalization of production on the banking sector. Accordingly, by 1965 '13 US banks had 211 branches overseas with nearly $9 billion in assets up from $3.5 billion five years earlier' (p. 44).
14. The main types of these institutional investors are pension funds, life insurance companies and forms of mutual funds. Trading desks of financial institutions and corporate treasury operations could also be considered as institutional investors (Davis and Steil 2001: 14). Pension funds collect and invest funds contributed by sponsors and beneficiaries for future pension entitlements. Life insurance companies are another type of long-term institutional investor, holding large shares of tradable asset portfolios, while mutual funds are vehicles to pool assets for financial investment purposes. The growth of 'defined contribution pension plans' increased the fraction of savings channeled through mutual and pension funds. This created a large and powerful constituency of financial investors able to affect corporate governance.
15. Toporowski also details the relationship between the rise of funded pension funds and the disintermediation from the banking system (2000: 50 onwards).
16. While Holmstrom and Kaplan (2001) argue, along with the mainstream literature, that this led to positive outcomes by reversing ill-advised diversification, lowering excess capacity and disciplining managers, Crotty and Goldstein (1993) find that takeover and buyout movement of the 1980s achieved little in efficiency gains.
17. Hostile bids are usually defined as bids that are pursued without the consent of target managements.
18. Agencies such as Standard and Poor's and Moody's rate corporate bonds. Triple A is the highest rating that goes to the companies with the strongest balance sheets and credit history. When these companies issue bonds in order to raise debt capital, the rate of interest on their bonds is usually not much higher than that of 'risk-free' US Treasury bonds. A bond that is issued as investment grade (rated higher than Ba1 by Moody's) but is later downgraded due to a perceived deterioration in the company's condition trades at a discount from its par value.

4. Perspectives on financialization

As documented by the empirical trends presented in Chapter 2, fundamental transformations have taken place that, in the post-1980 era, placed finance in a more prominent position than in the earlier post-World War II period. These changes provoked a number of scholars to pay specific attention to issues related to these transformations. Now, there is a growing literature that deals with different aspects of the financialization phenomenon and includes contributions from a variety of perspectives. In this chapter, I use these contributions in an attempt to uncover how much we know about financialization and how our conception of the phenomenon can be enhanced. Building on the insights of these contributions, I then construct an initial framework to understand the main aspects of the financialization process in the light of the historical discussion of the previous chapter.

Broadly, I identify three types of approach to the financialization phenomenon.[1] The first can be called the 'long-waves approach', best represented by the works of Arrighi (1994, 2003 and 2005) and his co-authors who evaluate the financialization era within a context of recurring long waves of capitalist history. According to this literature, each long cycle of capitalism consists of two segments: an increase in material production followed by a crisis due to overaccumulation and a financial expansion cycle. The post-1980 era represents this financial expansion cycle of the latest long wave of the capitalist system. Second, a diverse set of works analyse financialization as part of the structural changes associated with neoliberalism after 1980. Crotty (2005), Duménil and Lévy (2004a, b, c, 2005), Harvey (2003, 2005), Sweezy (1997), Amin (1996, 2003), and Panitch and Gindin (2004, 2005) are among the leading authors who discuss the financialization process within the context of the neoliberal structural changes. Although these authors have differing explanations regarding the causes and consequences of financialization, they all see it as part of a broader set of global economic phenomena. A third set of authors focus more specifically on the changing role of financial markets as it relates to the governance of NFCs. Lazonick and O'Sullivan (2000), Froud et al. (2000, 2002a, b), various authors from the regulation school and Stockhammer (2004) discuss corporate governance changes and their consequences. Below I discuss the main points raised by all three of these

approaches while highlighting some of the major questions left unanswered in the debates.

LONG WAVES OF CAPITALISM

While the review of Morgan House and the dominance of finance in the
late 19th century brought up interesting similarities and differences
between the current era of financial expansion and the one at the end of the
19th century, the long waves approach goes beyond that and emphasizes the
similarities between today's financial expansion and a number of others,
going back as far as the 14th century. Arrighi, the leading scholar in this
tradition, first draws attention to the rise of financialization in *The Long
Twentieth Century*, where he focuses on the bifurcation of trade-based
accumulation and financial expansion as well as the geopolitics of global
finance. Throughout various works, he attempts to place financialization
within a story of long cycles of capitalist development. According to
Arrighi (1994, 2003 and 2005) and Arrighi and Silver (1999), since the
1400s the 'world system' has passed through four cycles. Each cycle was led
by a hegemonic power, which started losing its strength at the end of the
cycle and the road was opened for the rise of a new one. From this perspective, four 'systemic cycles of accumulation' are identified: the Genoese
cycle of the 15th century to the early 17th century; the Dutch cycle of the
late 16th century through the 18th century, the British cycle of the latter
half of the 18th century through to the early 20th century; and the US cycle
of the 19th century to the present.[2]

At the end of each cycle, a worldwide crisis of accumulation occurs,
leading to a crisis of hegemony as the economy of the previous hegemonic
power is surpassed by the next one. During these repeated hegemonic crises,
the following three phenomena are observed. First, rivalries among leading
powers are intensified. Second, a financial expansion that is centered
around the hegemonic power in decline is observed. And third, a new locus
of power within the world economy begins to emerge (ibid.: 65). Arrighi

Table 4.1   Arrighi's long centuries

Time period	Hegemonic power
1450–1600s	Genoese
1600s–late 1700s	Dutch
Late 1700s–early 1900s	British
Early 1900s–2000s	United States

et al. (1999) argue that we can observe all three of these in the last couple of decades although the current crisis is not necessarily an exact replica of the previous ones. What makes the current financialization era peculiar is the far more rapid and conspicuous development of financialization compared with the earlier financial expansions (p. 88).

For the long waves perspective, these financial expansions are repeated throughout capitalist history and are only transitions to the next cycle, not a final phase. Hilferding ([1910] 1985) and Lenin's ([1916] 1988) analyses, which saw 'finance capital' as the latest stage of capitalism, are dismissed by Arrighi. While Hilferding's ([1910] 1985) analysis led to a conclusion that 'finance capital' in itself could to a certain extent provide an economically stable regime in which a small number of giant banks could essentially control an economy based on powerful oligopolies in core industries, Lenin ([1916] 1988) claimed that 'finance capital' would be the final stage of capitalist development and would end because of the global imperialist war and the revolutions it would trigger, not from primarily internal contradictions as an economic system.[3] Hence, Hilferding ([1910] 1985) and Lenin ([1916] 1988) theorized not only this first (or in Arrighi's terms the third) 'finance capital' regime, but also a final stage of capitalism rather than a phase of an ever-repeating cycle of a real sector-dominated competitive phase followed by a finance-dominated oligopoly phase. In *The Long Twentieth Century* Arrighi argues that '[f]inance capital is not a particular stage of world capitalism, let alone its latest and highest stage. Rather, it is a recurrent phenomenon' (1994: ix). And Arrighi and Silver (1999) argue that 'global financial expansion of the last 20 years or so is neither a new stage of world capitalism nor the harbinger of a 'coming hegemony of global markets.' Rather, it is the clearest sign that we are in the midst of a hegemonic crisis' (p. 272).

Within this framework of long waves, recurrences of financial expansions at the final phases of long cycles are one of the main expressions of a certain unity within the history of capitalism. Arrighi, following Braudel, identifies the beginning of financial expansions with 'the moment when the leading business agencies of the preceding trade expansions switch their energies and resources from the commodity to money trades' (p. 86). Arrighi (1994, 2003, 2005) and Arrighi and Silver (1999) argue that the resemblance between financialization of the current era and past financial expansions represent a continuity within the history of capitalism. Then the question becomes why do financial expansions occur; how and why do the leading NFCs shift their use of resources to financial operations? Arrighi and Silver (1999) argue that these developments are the outcome of two main tendencies inherent in the capitalist system: overaccumulation of capital and intense competition among states for mobile capital.[4]

Overaccumulation of capital is reflected as an exhaustion of profitable investment opportunities in the real sector, which is preceded by an increased competition in product markets. This, Arrighi argues, drives the nonfinancial entities within the system towards more involvement in financial businesses:

> When escalating competition reduces the availability of relatively empty, profitable niches in the commodity markets, the leading capitalist organizations have one last refuge, to which they can retreat and shift competitive pressures onto others. This final refuge is the money market – in Schumpeter's words, 'always, as it were, the headquarters of the capitalist system, from which orders go out to its individual divisions' [Schumpeter (1961: 126)] (Arrighi 1994: 50).

Note that as the source of the troubles in the productive sector, the increase in the degree of competition is pointed out by Arrighi. As we will see below, this approach is in contrast with the 'monopoly capital school' stagnationist explanation of financial expansions.

Furthermore, Arrighi (2003) points out that the scale of financial expansions grows to encompass the whole world during this phase. Hence, the financial expansion is never limited solely to the leading hegemon's economy. Accordingly, worldwide financial liberalization, the opening up of capital markets and similar developments should all be considered as part of this expansion. All these developments in this phase also have contradictory effects on the stability of the system. Arrighi (2003) argues that financialization destabilizes the very order it is supposed to stabilize; first, by worsening realization problems; second, by undermining the power of the hegemonic state; and third, by provoking resistance and rebellion among the groups subordinated to finance:

> The main reason for anticipating a new debacle is that financial expansions have a fundamentally contradictory impact on systemic stability. In the short run – with the understanding that, in this context, a short run encompasses decades rather than years – financial expansions tend to stabilize the existing order, by enabling incumbent hegemonic groups to shift onto subordinate groups, nationally and internationally, the burdens of the intensifying competition that challenges their hegemony. (Arrighi 2003: 68)

In turning to an analysis of the potential sources of instability during a financial expansion, Arrighi changes the unit of analysis from 'leading capitalist organizations' to 'leading capitalist states.' It is not clear though whether this is due simply to a conflation of the interests of the leading capitalist organizations and hegemonic states. Unfortunately, Arrighi is not helpful in distinguishing between leading economic and political organizations. However, with this new unit of analysis the effect of financialization is to shift competitive pressures from the hegemonic power onto other nations.[5] Apart from the instability created due to hegemonic shifts and due to social and political processes, there are economic sources of instability during financial expansions:

> Economically, such expansions systematically divert purchasing power from demand-creating investment in commodities (including labor power) to hoarding and speculation, thereby exacerbating realization problems. Politically, they tend to be associated with the emergence of new configurations of power, which undermine the capacity of the incumbent hegemonic state to turn to its advantage the system-wide intensification of competition. And socially, the massive redistribution of rewards and the social dislocations entailed by financial expansions tend to provoke movements of resistance and rebellion among subordinate groups and strata, whose established ways of life are coming under attack. (ibid.)

Destabilizing trends that come with financial expansions find their origin in rising income inequality which diverts resources away from demand-creating venues. Hence, rising income inequality becomes a cause of an ultimate crisis during financial expansions by transferring purchasing power away from demand-creating activities to financial activities and speculation. When we look at the US economy, we see that since the 1980s total debt across sectors has been rising and this rise has had a positive effect on aggregate demand while other aspects of the neoliberal era have caused a decline in it,[6] a point that I will come back to in the next section.

Returning to the issue of a hegemonic crisis, Arrighi's argument that financialization signals a transition from one regime of accumulation on a world scale to another is based on Braudel's thesis that the stage of financial expansions are 'a sign of autumn' in that they announce the maturity of the major capitalist developments (Braudel 1984: 246). Arrighi and Silver (1999) argue that the US now has a greater potential than Britain did to preserve its declining hegemony through 'exploitative domination,' which includes both taking advantage of financial flows into the US and the use of military power to secure resources. Accordingly, there are two possibilities. Either the US adjusts and accommodates the rising economic power of the East Asia region, in which case a transition to a new world order would be relatively painless; or it resists adjustment and accommodation and leads the system to a breakdown. Arrighi and Silver summarize this approach as follows:

> What lies in front of us are the difficulties involved in transforming the modern world into a commonwealth of civilizations that reflects the changing balance of power between Western and non-Western civilizations, first and foremost the reemerging China-centered civilization. How drastic and painful the transformation is going to be – and, indeed, whether it will eventually result in a

commonwealth rather than in the mutual destruction of the world's civiliza-
tions – ultimately depends on two conditions. It depends, first, on how intelli-
gently the main centers of Western civilization can adjust to a less exalted status
and, second, on whether the main centers of reemerging China-centered civilization can collectively rise up to the task of providing system-level solutions to
the system-level problems left behind by US hegemony. (1999: 286)[7]

Leaving aside the issues of hegemonic transition, Arrighi's explanation
of financialization as a result of overaccumulation of capital raises two
important questions. First, how can the leading capitalist organizations
retreat to the financial realm and shift competitive pressures onto others?
It is not clear, for example, why certain NFCs can move to the financial
sector and shift competitive pressures onto others, while the others cannot
make a similar move. Two possibilities come to mind. First, if profitability
in the financial sector is higher, regardless of the reasons behind this, the
firm that moves to the financial realm could support its total profits by
profits from financial operations and gain an edge against its competitors.
The second possibility is to use financial operations to support real operations, thereby gaining a competitive advantage. This could be seen in, for
example, General Motors's use of its financial division, GMAC, to provide
support for its sales, as discussed in the earlier chapter. But then, of course,
there is the question of why, if it is possible to retreat to the financial realm,
would some enterprises not be able to accomplish this retreat. Although
Arrighi does not provide an answer to this question, in order to acquire a
more concrete understanding of the financialization process we need to
unravel the reasons behind why and how NFCs move towards financial
businesses. If we follow the General Motors example, we do see that other
firms in the same industry could indeed switch to financial operations
which they could use to support their real operations.

Second, Arrighi does not explain why financial markets have high rates of
return when profits in the real sector are low due to the overaccumulation
problems here. As Figure 4.1 demonstrates, in the US economy, average
NFC profitability began its decline in the late 1970s, while, as Figure 2.2
showed, financial corporations' profitability with respect to NFC profitability began increasing after 1985. This was around the time (see Figure 4.1)
when NFC before-tax profits reached a low and started to gradually rise
again. Within Arrighi's framework, during the phase of financial expansions, financial assets are supposed to have higher rates of return thus
leading the NFCs to engagement in financial activities. However, the production and trade of goods and services do not stop because of this. Arrighi
does not provide an explanation for the continuation of their nonfinancial
activities despite the overaccumulation/profitability problems. There are two
possibilities. One, there is some sort of equalization regarding the two profit

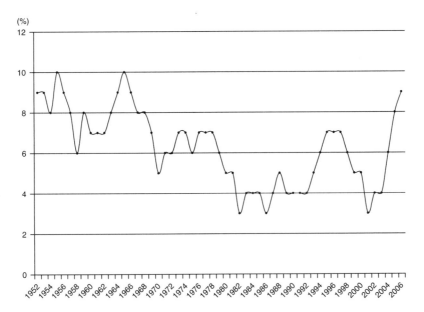

Source: FFA Tables B.102 and F.102.

Figure 4.1 *NFC profits before tax as a percent of tangible assets,*
1952–2006

rates. Or NFCs cannot easily get out of their investments in the real sector
(Crotty 1993).

These questions are directly related to the question of the sources of
financial profits and deserve special attention. It is not clear in Arrighi's
analysis whether finance is seen as just another venue for the capitalist to
create value when troubles accumulate in the industrial site, or whether the
financial sphere is where claims to value that has already been produced or
that is to be produced in the future, are distributed. Pollin (1996) rightly
points out this lack of clarity in the analysis and provides a thorough critique of this approach, especially in regards to Arrighi's use of Marx's 'cir-
cuits of capital' to describe the real and financial expansion cycles of the
long waves. If there are no additional profits in the real sector, firms will
only distribute existing profits among themselves in a zero-sum game. It is
also possible that financial operations serve as a redistribution of income
and wealth towards these capitalists. The final alternative is that increased
financialization helps to raise the profitability of real activities which pre-
sumably would improve the profitability of financial intermediaries in
return. Of course, financial profits could also be created on paper due to

speculative increases in assets. However, these speculative profits would not have a counterpart on the output side. Hence, spending these 'paper' profits would potentially lead to excess aggregate demand and inflation. Furthermore, large-scale selling of financial assets to realize these speculative profits would cause a fall in their prices and lead to the disappearance of those speculative profits. Although in his reply to Pollin's critique, Arrighi does spend more time in attempting to explain the sources of financial profitability, there is still plenty of room within his framework to show the mechanisms.[8]

Overall, Arrighi's approach has the merit of bringing in history and a long-term perspective to the discussions of financialization. Nevertheless, he does not provide a satisfactory explanation of the interconnections of the phenomenon he observes. Although financialization is a result of the overaccumulation of capital and the resulting crisis of hegemony, the mechanisms of switching to a new hegemonic regime are not clear. Despite his attempt to provide a sweeping historical perspective, as Pollin (1996) put it, he does not answer the question of 'what exactly are financial expansions, and in what ways do they operate as cause or effect during historical transitions' (p. 114). Part of this problem arises from the fact that he does not give a satisfactory explanation of the sources of financial expansions and profits. However, as it will become clear later in this chapter, Arrighi is not the only one who fails to explain certain key relationships. However, bringing together insights from all these perspectives can help us in constructing an understanding of the phenomenon. Furthermore, the theme of overaccumulation of capital appears, albeit in different forms, throughout most works on financialization.

Some of these works directly use Arrighi's framework. For example, Krippner (2005) attempts to concretize Arrighi's thesis by focusing on the changing nature of NFC incomes in the US. She provides an empirical demonstration of the rise of financial incomes as a percent of the total income of the NFCs. Krippner analyses IRS tax return data to identify the financialization trends in the US economy. To that end, she adopts Arrighi's approach and defines financialization as a 'pattern of accumulation in which profits accrue primarily through financial channels rather than through trade and commodity production' (p. 174). She does not dwell on the theoretical discussion regarding the rise of finance and financial profits but instead, through a careful analysis of the US data, identifies an increasing upward trend in NFCs' portfolio income – defined as the sum of interest income, dividend income and capital gains.[9] She finds a trend similar to the one depicted in Figure 2.10 above. Financial incomes of NFCs started increasing in the 1970s and reached new heights in the 1980s and 1990s according to Krippner's study and as was shown in Figure 2.10. While Krippner (2005) presents an ambitious empirical documentation of the financialization trends in the nonfinancial corporate sector and provides us with detailed statistics, she leaves unanswered the question of why we observe such an increase in financial investments of NFCs. She does show, though, that outsourcing, subsidiary formation and increased global incomes of these corporations do not lie behind the rise of their financial incomes. Moreover, on the question of the sources of financial profits she identifies the magnitudes of three categories of financial incomes: interest income, dividends and capital gains. Hence, her empirical focus and the detailed data presented in her work serve to bolster the case for the extent and importance of the financialization of the US economy.

FINANCIALIZATION AND NEOLIBERALISM

Financialization can also be seen as an integral part of the neoliberal economic structures. Following the economic instability of the 1970s a new set of economic policies started to be implemented in much of the world. These policies aimed to reduce the government intervention and regulation in all sorts of economic activities and leave an increasing portion of the economic activities to the 'free markets.' The financial expansion of the last decades hence was accompanied by the widespread adoption of these policies, generally referred as neoliberalism:

> Neoliberalism is in the first instance a theory of political economic practices that proposes that human well-being can best be advanced by liberating individual entrepreneurial freedoms and skills within an institutional framework characterized by strong private property rights, free markets, and free trade. The role of the state is to create and preserve an institutional framework appropriate to such practices. (Harvey 2005: 2)

Crotty (2005) stresses the importance of considering the spread of neoliberal policies and the changes in financial markets as these two developments created a paradox: first, a slowdown in the rate of global aggregate demand growth and an increasing intensity of competition in key product markets that lowers average profit rates; and second, a shift from patient financial markets that seek long-term growth to impatient financial markets that raise real interest rates, force NFCs to pay an increasing share of their income to financial agents while drastically changing managerial incentives and shortening the planning horizons of NFCs.

Within this 'neoliberal paradox,' not only does financialization shorten the time horizons of NFCs and induce them to pump out cash flow, but also simultaneously the neoliberal regime creates destructive competition and lowers profit rates, so that it has much more pernicious effects than just those of financialization considered separately. This paradox is 'deeply rooted in the structures and practices of neoliberalism', according to Crotty (2005: 79). These structures and practices brought six constraints on the global demand and hence constituted the first part of the 'neoliberal paradox':

1. Slow growth of employment, real wages and mass consumption.
2. High real interest rates, and rapidly rising household and business debt burdens that initially raise but eventually restrict demand growth.
3. Increasingly restrictive national fiscal policy after the 1980s.
4. Slower growth in gross private domestic investment worldwide.
5. The spread of IMF 'austerity' programs and World Bank 'structural adjustment' programs across the globe.
6. The weakening of most of the high-growth East Asian late-development models in the wake of the 1997 Asian financial crisis. (2005: 79–80)[10]

The other side of the paradox is rooted in the changes that took place in the financial markets and in their relationship to the rest of the economy. The turning point was the shift to extremely restrictive monetary policy in the early 1980s, which raised real interest rates and shortened the payback period used to evaluate potential investment projects (Crotty 2002: 18). In the same period, managers 'began to think of their own subunits as liquid assets that could be disgorged to capital markets if they underperformed and to look at other firms as assets to be added to their own portfolio if their acquisition would raise expected returns' (ibid.: 20). This shift to a portfolio view of nonfinancial firms was completed by the hostile takeover movement of the 1980s:

> The late 1970s saw conglomeration fall out of favor with financial investors, but in the 1980s the US stock market became, for the first time in the post war era, a well functioning 'market for corporate control.'. . . Raiders relied primarily on debt to finance takeovers, pushing NFC indebtedness to historic highs.
> What the 1980s takeover movement did accomplish was to force the financial or portfolio view of the firm on NFC management. . . . These developments accelerated the ongoing process of the shortening of NFC planning horizons caused by destructive product market competition. (ibid.: 20–1)

While this financial conception of the firm was gaining ground, the influence of institutional investors on stock prices and management behavior increased. This was followed by the internalization within NFCs' top management of the pressure to push stock prices ever higher as a result of the 'shareholder value' movement. All these developments led to changes in the behavior of NFCs described by Crotty:

Many NFCs responded to the low profits and high costs of external funds they faced in much of the 1980s and 1990s, as well as to the high returns they observed being made on financial assets and financial enterprises, in two innovative ways. First, an increasing percent of NFC investment funds were used to acquire financial assets. Second, firms created or bought financial subsidiaries, and expanded those financial subsidiaries already in existence. (2002: 34)

The Role of the Accumulation Crisis

Harvey (2003) also emphasizes that financialization is part of a regime switch from the regulated economy of the 'Golden Age' to a neoliberal regime in a way similar to that of Crotty and as we will see below, to Duménil and Lévy; while also making use of concepts such as the shift in hegemony borrowed from Arrighi. What was the driving force behind this financialization and neoliberalization process? According to Harvey (2003), financialization is not itself a new accumulation regime, but is part of a wide range of developments in the post-1980 era including the shift in the US economy towards offshoring and its transformation into a service and rentier economy. The rising influence of financial markets in economic activity was accompanied by a rising involvement of NFCs in financial businesses (Harvey 2005: 32).

Harvey brings together the two strands of explanation as to the causes of financialization and argues that there are two related but distinct factors that explain the rise of finance in the post-1980 era. On the one hand, an 'overaccumulation of capital' leads to a shrinkage of profitable investment opportunities and hence requires a temporal and spatial reshuffling of the processes of production and accumulation.[11] The overaccumulation of capital requires a redirection of investments towards more profitable parts of the world and/or postponing investments. According to Harvey, financialization helps this 'spatio-temporal fix' by redirecting capital flows from one space to another (2003: 122). On the other hand, political decisions have been effective in moving finance capital to the center-stage in the post-1970s world through financial liberalization and deregulation. Moreover, financialization has been effective in restoring capitalist class power in general as financial markets provided the means to procure and concentrate wealth (2005: 90). This is a point stressed by Duménil and Lévy (2004c), who show that in the era of financialization, income shares of the top segments of society, including the top executives of NFCs, has increased tremendously. Before discussing the second part of this explanation, let us first ask how overaccumulation of capital would lead to financialization.

Harvey's approach to financialization helps to highlight the contribution of both structural and political factors in the drive towards it. However, he does not go beyond providing a general framework of financialization. Specifically, he falls short of demonstrating how it can help (or has helped) overcome the overaccumulation problem. Amin (1996, 2003) also presents a similar analysis in which financialization can be seen as a reflection of ongoing problems in the real economy as well as a mechanism to manage the structural crisis of capitalism.[12] In this sense, financialization is not a new phase of capitalism but rather a transitory phenomenon, as Arrighi similarly argues. It is the product of the crisis in which capital surplus cannot be utilized for the expansion of productive systems. The crisis of the capitalist system is defined by an overall imbalance between supply and demand in the sense that a growing share of the surplus created cannot find profitable real investment outlets. This thesis is similar to the monopoly capital argument that I will discuss shortly. According to Amin (2003), the reason behind the crisis is the tendency for the rate of profit to decline. This prompts the owners of capital to either postpone their investment or try to find ways to increase their competitiveness. Amin argues that an alternative outlet in the form of 'financial investment' is therefore created as a way of managing this crisis:

> The crisis was expressed in the fact that profits derived from exploitation did not find sufficient investment outlets likely to develop productive capacity. Management of the crisis therefore consisted in finding other outlets for the surplus of floating capital, so that it did not suddenly undergo a massive loss of value. (Amin 2003: 16)

Thus, Amin provides one answer to the question of why the profit rate in financial markets and on financial assets could be higher and remain high for a while. According to him, the answer is a speculative appreciation in the prices of financial assets. This resulted in what Amin (2003) calls a 'financial hypertrophy' which includes:

> a volume of capital markets expanding at a rate far above that of economic growth . . .; an extraordinary diversification of the arrangement and instruments available on these markets . . .; the growing weight of finance in corporate affairs, as financial investment outside the company takes an increasing share of resources in comparison with investment in physical assets . . .; progressive globalization of the financial hypertrophy, expressed in stock-market capitalization in so-called 'emerging' economies. (Amin 2003: 43)

Hence, the growth of financial investments at a rate that is out of proportion with real investments creates a financial bubble. Again, this is accompanied by an increased potential for fragility as the financial bubble cannot go on forever. According to Amin, financialization essentially depends on asset price inflation, which creates a bubble – a similar point to that of Sweezy

(1997) and Magdoff and Sweezy (1987). Only a solution to the accumulation crisis in the real sector would create the conditions for a renewal of vigorous growth and eliminate financialization and the bubble. However, he goes on to argue, there is no sign of such a solution and financialization continues through a bifurcation of profit rates (low for real investment, high for financial investment) (p. 51).

For Amin, it is still possible to see some permanent features of capitalism emerging out of financialization. He claims that in a post-financialization era it is possible to imagine that the relationship between productive capital and financial markets and instruments will be fundamentally different from those that existed in the pre-financialization era (Amin 2003: 52). Having said this, he does not speculate on the future of financial markets and instruments and how they will relate to productive capital.[13] Amin essentially argues that NFCs faced with a problem of insufficient real investment outlets directed their funds into the financial sphere. However, his overall analysis also fails to give an account of how the NFCs made a transition to investing in financial assets instead of real assets. We are still faced with the problem of how the transition is made and how initially low profitability in the real sector would create higher profitability in the financial sector, a problem that the authors discussed earlier but have not answered in a satisfactory way. However, another interesting question emerges out of this discussion regarding the reasons behind the overaccumulation crisis which I will briefly discuss before moving onto the role of politics.

Competition or Concentration?

While Arrighi traces the roots of overaccumulation problems and financialization to increased competition in product markets and others such as Harvey talk about the implications of increased international competition, especially for the US manufacturing sector, Sweezy (1997) makes the exact opposite argument. In a brief discussion of the subject, he points to the rise of 'monopoly capital' as providing the impetus for financialization. He argues that financialization is one of the most important trends in the recent history of capitalism and that it is a result of the monopolization of capital – the proliferation of monopolistic/oligopolistic multinational corporations. Unlike Arrighi, Sweezy sees this as part of a long-term slowdown of capitalist development, not a recurring long cycle, though it should also be noted that Sweezy only focuses on the post-war period in his analysis.

According to Sweezy, monopolization generates an increasing flow of profits on the one hand, while on the other hand it reduces the demand for additional real investment because greater capacity would lower industry profits. The lack of profitable outlets in real capital formation due to monopolization and a dearth of big technical innovations, rather than increased competition, lead to financialization. The end result is that funds get diverted to 'purely financial and mostly speculative channels.' This explanation of financialization again begs an answer to the question of where financial profits come from when real profitability is declining, a question that also emerged in Arrighi's discussion.

The general framework of the 'monopoly capital' approach to finance can be found in Magdoff and Sweezy (1987) (see especially Part II).[14] The key difference in this analysis lies in the emphasis on the idea that financialization does not provide any solution to the problem of the lack of profitable investment outlets. There is neither a shift in hegemony, nor a relocation of capital in time and space. Rather, financialization creates an inflationary phase in the financial sector which could go on as long as investors have confidence in financial asset price appreciation:

> [in the financial sector] there is plenty of money available (cash plus unused credit), and hunger for profits added to competitive pressures drives all financial enterprises to put as much of it as possible to work. This generates an upward tendency in the price of financial instruments which in turn sparks a speculative psychology which comes to pervade the financial community and provide its own justification. (p. 104)

It is not clear though how financial enterprises would dispose of the accumulating cash and unused credit especially if the monopolized real sector does not need to borrow due to a lack of profitable investment opportunities. While there is a plethora of literature on the financial asset bubbles of the post-1980 era, especially the long boom of the stock market in the 1990s, Sweezy's essential suggestion of a link between monopolization and financialization has not been empirically analysed. A simple look at the NFC profitability and financialization figures indicate that the decline in the profitability of NFCs occurred in the 1970s; however the boom in financial markets and activities came after the early 1980s, when foreign competition had been increasing for the NFCs. Therefore, it seems that Sweezy's thesis that financialization is the result of the monopolization process needs further empirical examination.

Politics of Financialization

The accumulation crisis that unfolded in the 1970s created the structural reasons and the basis for a shift in the economic policy sphere. Within the new neoliberal regime, finance gained the upper hand. Financialization, according to Harvey, is an integral part of the neoliberal regime in that this new regime 'entailed shifting the balance of power and interests within the bourgeoisie from production activities to institutions of finance capital' (Harvey 2003: 63). However, we are faced with the question of whether it is possible to distinguish between the representatives of financial and industrial capital. Duménil and Lévy provide an answer to this question by arguing that the term 'finance capitalists' should not only designate the owners of finance capital but also encompass the upper fraction of the wealthiest capitalists. For example, top managers of NFCs have become super rich in the neoliberal era mostly through stock options, that is, as rentiers. Thus, a key element of the rentier class is now in the nonfinancial sector, complicating the earlier distinction of financial versus industrial capitalists. Then, financialized neoliberal regime can be seen as

> the expression of the desire of a class of capitalist owners and institutions in which their power is concentrated, which we collectively call 'finance,' to restore – in the context of a general decline in popular struggles – the class's revenues and power, which had diminished since the Great Depression and World War II. Far from being inevitable, this was a political action. (Harvey 2003: 2)

This brings us back to the political background of the changes made which enabled a rise in the size and power of finance. The Federal Reserve's raising of the interest rates at the end of the 1970s is labeled as the 'coup of 1979' by Duménil and Lévy (2005: 14). They note that '[t]he upper fraction of finance fought constantly for the restoration of its privileges and preeminence, in particular concerning its international activities' (2005: 24). This sudden rise in interest rates in 1979 marks the origins of rising financial sector profitability. At the same time, it denotes the beginning of the current period of deregulation and return to 'free market' economics. This, according to Duménil and Lévy, was a deliberate policy choice, imposed by finance capital and its representatives in government rather than just the standard government macro policy response to rising inflation. Macroeconomic conditions of the late 1970s, gave finance capital the chance to push its agenda.

This argument is also supported by the literature that analyses political developments behind the financial liberalization and deregulation process. For example, Kuttner (1997) draws attention to the political aspects of the deregulation process more concretely by summarizing the political and lobbying activities of the finance industry (see p. 173 onwards). He argues that:

> the repeal of Regulation Q and the competition with money-market mutual funds produced a new set of pressures for entrepreneurial, go-go banking. The result was a series of highly speculative investments. . . . And it led the financial

industry to lobby Congress, successfully for the most part, for deregulation on a broad front, in order to permit the kind of high-yield investments that the banks needed. (p. 173)

Isenberg (2000) points out that '[t]he current de-regulation has fostered finance's transformation from being an input into the production process to being an independent industry that innovates and sells its own products' (p. 266). Hence, financial market liberalization and deregulation reflected a general increase in the size and power of finance. By the removal of the checks and controls on most financial activities, finance became more powerful, not only in terms of the expansion of financial activities and markets, but also in terms of political influence, which in turn helped them to further liberalize and deregulate financial markets.

Hence, we can conclude that the rise of the financialized neoliberal regime was not necessarily the only available road following the accumulation crisis of the 1970s but it was in many aspects the result of deliberate policy interventions in the benefit of the wealthier capitalists.[15]

Financialization and Hegemony Reconsidered

Coming back to Harvey's theorization of neoliberalism and financialization, we see that he also argues that by the 1980s or so the US manufacturing sector, faced with intense international competition, lost its hegemonic position. This is similar to Arrighi's explanation of the financial expansion, except that for Harvey it is the outcome of structural factors as much as of political design. Harvey agrees with Arrighi on the issue of declining American hegemony but argues that the US continued to assert its hegemony through finance:

> In those areas where US firms remained powerful, the turn to offshore production of components or even whole products placed more and more productive capacity outside the borders of the United States even though the repatriation of profits kept wealth flowing towards it. In other areas, the monopoly privileges that attach to patented technologies and licensing laws gave welcome relief from the draining away of US dominance in production. The US was moving towards becoming a rentier economy in relation to the rest of the world and a service economy at home. (Harvey, 2003: 65–6)

The idea that finance has played a key role in securing the hegemony of the US on a global scale is also shared by other authors such as Gowan (1999), Panitch and Gindin (2004), and Hudson (2003). Harvey returns to this issue in discussing the international features of the financial system in the neoliberal era. The following long quote from him properly explains the role of finance in the neoliberal order:

Internationally, finance capital proved more and more volatile and predatory. Various bouts of devaluation and destruction of capital were visited (usually through the good graces of IMF structural adjustment programmes) as an antidote to the inability to keep capital accumulation going smoothly by expanded reproduction. In some instances, for example in Latin America in the 1980s, whole economies were raided and their assets recovered by US finance capital. In others, it was more simply an export of devaluation. The hedge funds' attack upon Thai and Indonesian currencies in 1997, backed up by the savage deflationary policies demanded by the IMF, drove even viable concerns into bankruptcy throughout East and South-East Asia. Unemployment and impoverishment were the result for millions of people. That crisis also conveniently sparked a flight to the dollar, confirming Wall Street's dominance and generating an amazing boom in asset values for the affluent in the United States. Class struggles began to coalesce around issues such as IMF-imposed structural adjustment, the predatory activities of finance capital, and the loss of rights through privatization. The tone of anti-imperialism began to shift towards antagonism to the main agents of financialization – the IMF and the World Bank being frequently singled out. (Harvey, 2003: 66)

Financial power has thus been used in order to further the neoliberal agenda. Financialization became a tool to appropriate assets of 'developing countries' and forced further liberalization and deregulation of these economies. Furthermore, it also contributed to an increased frequency of financial crises in many parts of the world, which in turn were used to earn quick returns for finance capital while forcing these countries to accept the neoliberal regime. In short, international financial capital has a dominant position within the neoliberal capitalist system and pushes for 'rules of the game' that are to its advantage, such as capital-account liberalization. Governments in 'developed' countries and multilateral institutions, which are themselves closely interlocked with international financial capital, are complicit partners in this process.

Rise of Finance: Parasites or Saviors?

The next important question is about the consequences of the financialized neoliberal regime in relation to economic performance in general. Crotty (2005) argues that as a result of the 'neoliberal paradox,' we observe that the combined effects of the slowdown in the rate of global aggregate demand growth and an increasing intensity of competition in key product markets together with financialization lowered NFC profit rates, raised NFC indebtedness, slowed the rate of capital accumulation and forced NFC top management to switch to short-term 'survivalist' strategies that involved attacks on white and blue collar labor and on key firm suppliers. At the same time, financial markets forced NFCs to discharge greater shares of their funds in the forms of higher interest and dividend payments and stock buybacks. These resulted in the further slowdown of aggregate demand growth: '. . . neoliberal globalization is also destroying conditions in both product and financial markets that are necessary for the successful long-term performance of large nonfinancial firms' (Crotty 2005: 107).

This approach is complemented by Duménil and Lévy (2004a, b, c, and 2005), who also provide historical accounts of changes within past decades supported by empirical analysis; shed light on potential consequences of financialization on capital accumulation and income distribution; and demonstrate how financialization is related to other parts of the neoliberal economic order. On the question of the performance of the nonfinancial sector in the face of the financialization and neoliberalization trends, Duménil and Lévy (2004a, 2004b) analyse the real and financial components of profitability in the US between 1952 and 2000. A key finding of their analysis in relation to finance is that the rate of profit in the financial sector remained relatively low during the Keynesian policy era, while it soared during the neoliberal decades, a finding similar to the trends shown earlier in Figures 2.1, 2.2 and 2.3. They argue that this illustrates how finance was subordinated to the real sector until the end of the 1970s. Duménil and Lévy go on to posit a conflict between the interests of finance and industrial capital, claiming that the increase in financial profits came at the expense of the profits of industrial capital. They note that the rate of capital accumulation is closely related to the rate of retained profits, that is, the rate of profit after payment of interest and dividends. By forcing an increase in interest and dividend payments, financialization left NFCs with fewer funds and contributed to a slowdown of investment in France and the United States (2004a: 119–120).

According to Harvey (2005), financialization had a dual effect on the US economy. While the shift towards financial power brought great direct benefits such as ever cheaper imported goods (p. 65), it had traumatic effects upon the industrial structure and contributed to offshore production and deindustrialization (p. 64). Although Harvey argues that financialization had negative impacts on capital accumulation in the US through deindustrialization, he does not elaborate on the mechanisms through which this happened. However, the implication is that financialization directed funds to parts of the world other than the US, be it due to cheaper labor or to expanding markets in those places. Hence, finance became a tool through which capital was shifted from one part of the world to another. Krippner (2005) showed that there is some empirical support for Harvey's thesis. According to her data, global financial incomes of NFCs have been increasing steadily since the early 1980s (p. 196).

Panitch and Gindin (2005) also discuss financialization in the context of neoliberal policies. However, while most of the literature focuses on the negative effects of financialization on growth and industry, Panitch and Gindin (2005) argue that financialization can help accumulation by imposing the closure of unprofitable businesses and by encouraging mergers and acquisitions, which expands capital's ability to exit.[16] They seem to accept that overaccumulation or 'chronic excess capacity' is an inherent problem of capitalism and they assert that financialization helps to solve this problem via the discipline it imposes. Contrary to the arguments that finance's increasing claims leave fewer funds retained for investment, they argue that:

> [t]he total surplus may be increased if finance disciplines firms to reorganize production, reallocates capital away from less profitable companies, helps to disseminate technology across sectors and generates the liquidity to supply venture capital to new businesses. . . . So even if the share claimed by finance increases, the net amount left for reinvestment may be higher than it would otherwise be. (p. 119)

This approach is in contrast with Dumenil and Lévy's claim that NFCs suffered from a decline in internal funds which slowed down their real capital accumulation. Although Duménil and Lévy empirically show the close correlation between internal funds and capital expenditures, Panitch and Gindin do not provide macro data to support their claims. Their framework is similar to the 'efficient markets hypothesis' in that the pressures brought by finance are seen as transferring funds from unprofitable businesses to profitable ones. Seccombe (2004) makes a similar argument. One of the significant outcomes of financialization and the ascendance of shareholder power has been a trend toward downsizing. This downsizing, negative social effects aside, is 'an essential corrective to capitalism's recurrent "tendency to over-production"' (p. 198). Seccombe (2004) also argues '[s]hort of wars and depressions, financial markets are vital to the Darwinian process of revitalizing the economy by culling laggards from the flock' (Seccombe 2004: 198). They do this by channeling funds into 'leading edge' technologies while abandoning the older plants and inefficient enterprises. This leads 'uncompetitive firms to renovate, sell out, or die' (ibid.). This argument is similar to Lazonick and O'Sullivan's (2000) argument that firms with long-term objectives and labor-management cooperation relations get destroyed in the short-run profit maximization game. A crucial difference is that Seccombe (2004) argues that this transformation gives rise to increased efficiency. Seccombe's claims find a similar reflection in Panitch and Gindin (2005):

> As for the implications of the relative increase in the role and power of financial institutions, there was an underestimation of how the deepening of capital

> markets, and the competitive pressures and mobility they generate, could lead to increased capital productivity and profit rates. They did this not just through their disciplinary impact on firms and governments, but also by reallocating capital and supporting the dissemination of technology across firms and sectors (more rapid exit of relatively inefficient firms, support for risky but innovative start-ups, dissemination of new technologies into old sectors). (p. 67)

The corporate scandals of the early 2000s and the collapse of the 'new economy' around the same time do not seem to get much attention within this framework. Moreover, to prove this point, empirical evidence is necessary either at macro or micro level. We need to know how much excess capacity has been shut down or whether excess capacity has been reduced or eliminated. However, none of these works presents no supporting empirical evidence to further these claims. Neither Panitch and Gindin (2005), nor Seccombe (2004) provide any empirical support for the argument that finance and the prominence of shareholder value helped overcome the chronic excess capacity of the system.

The larger share of overall profits that has recently gone to finance certainly includes speculative and rentier gains, but for Panitch and Gindin it may also be seen as representing in part a return for finance's contribution to keeping general profits higher than they would have otherwise been (2005: 68). They agree that there has been a slowdown in average annual growth rates, though they do not see this as a crisis for capitalism. They cite Maddison's long-run data to argue that growth rates are still above the average during 1820–1945 and that the 'productivity of capital' has been increasing (2005: 67). They go on to argue that the rate of accumulation would have been even lower if the new regime did not unleash financial forces, a thesis that cannot be empirically refuted since it is based on comparing a real regime with a hypothetical one. Although the argument that financialization helped to restore capitalist class power is common in the literature as discussed so far, it is not clear that it also helped capital accumulation in general. To take an example, financialization has destroyed industrial policy in many countries and helped end any chance of successful development, while it triggered financial crises across the world and led, through independent central banks and run-away options for financial interests, to high real interest rates and slower growth.

While Panitch and Gindin provide no evidence that financial markets have raised efficiency, Crotty and Goldstein (1993) discuss the question of whether US financial markets allocate credit efficiently in the context of the corporate restructuring of the 1980s and develop the argument that deregulated financial markets proved to be inefficient as credit allocators. Weller and Helppie (2002), also provide contrary evidence. They show that at least in the manufacturing sector: 'the stock market increase may have given lenders an incentive to invest primarily in companies that have seen large stock price gains, thereby possibly raising financial constraints for manufacturing firms' (p. 1). The channeling of funds into technology firms created significant levels of excess capacity in these industries, a result counter to the theses of Panitch and Gindin and Seccombe. Furthermore, Jürgens et al. (2002) find that, for the case of the European auto industry: 'shareholder value policy does not necessarily lead to better economic performance' (p. 61). Their analysis, on the contrary, shows that 'the more engaged companies are towards shareholder value policy, the less well they performed in terms of profit margins and returns on capital' (ibid.). Similarly, Carpenter et al. (2003) point out that for the companies in the optical network industry that used the advantageous stock market financing opportunities during the boom of 1998–2000, using their stock to accumulate innovative capability 'made them more vulnerable to the stock market collapse and the slowdown in the optical network industry in 2001–2003' (p. 963).[17] On this issue, Williams (2000) notes that the attempts by NFC managers in the 1990s to increase gains from increased labor productivity resulted in these gains being lost mostly to highly competitive product markets. As a result, most of the increases in the returns provided by the NFCs to stockholders came from rising share prices (p. 6).

The consequences of financialization are also discussed in the critical literature on corporate governance as we will see below. I will revisit this issue in more depth in the second part of the book when analysing the implications of the parallel rise in the financial incomes and payments of the NFCs for their investment behavior.

FINANCIAL MARKETS AND CORPORATE GOVERNANCE

A key feature of the financialized neoliberal regime for NFCs has been the changing nature of corporate governance theories and practices. As discussed above, in this era the long-term growth perspectives were replaced by an imperative to maximize shareholder value in the short-run. While mainstream finance and economics theories, specifically the 'agency theories,' hailed this transformation, a critical literature on corporate governance changes also emerged. As the home of these corporate governance changes was the US, most of the analysis focused on the US corporate governance structure. Nevertheless, critical studies on the changes in US corporate governance are not only significant in understanding the role of finance in the US economy, but are also helpful in contextualizing the promotion of US-style corporate governance in the 'developing countries' (Soederberg 2003;

Singh 2003; Glen et al. 2000). Since reviews of the mainstream agency theories are abundant, I will only briefly review them and discuss corporate governance from a more critical perspective.[18]

A significant part of the mainstream economics literature discusses corporate governance within the framework of 'agency theories.' Even though this literature is quite voluminous, its punch line is rather simple and straightforward, as Froud et al. describe it: '[T]he firm exists for the benefit of shareholders who own the firm and who should exercise control so that the interests of management are beneficially aligned with those of the owner shareholders around the pursuit of profit' (2002b: 5–6).

Most of the key ideas in this literature were developed in the 1970s. While NFCs were struggling with the adverse economic conditions of the 1970s and declining profitability, this new approach to corporate governance was being elaborated by a group of American financial economists. This approach later came to be known as 'agency theory' and played a crucial role in bringing about changes in corporate governance by providing an economic justification for them. This theory argued that having a takeover market that functioned as a market for corporate control would provide the necessary discipline for corporate managers to create higher profits. Jensen and Meckling (1976), and Fama and Jensen (1983a, b) established the foundations of this new literature which proposed new ways of conceptualizing the relationship between managers and investors. Agency theory argued that a corporation was a 'nexus of contracts' and its purpose was to allocate residual cash flows among managers, creditors and shareholders (Baskin and Miranti 1997: 259).

Corporate governance debates in general make a distinction between 'internal governance' and 'external governance' (Gillan 2006). The former includes the role of boards of directors, managerial incentives, and bylaws and charter provisions of the firms. External elements of firm governance includes laws, regulations and the institutional structure of capital markets (ownership structure) and labor market for the CEOs, board members and members of senior executive teams (ibid.). Much of this literature is directly concerned with the financial structure of the firm. While there are theories focusing on risk-sharing and taxation, the bulk of the literature suggests that the main function of the firm's financial structure is to mitigate managerial incentive problems (Jensen and Meckling 1976; Ross 1977; Grossman and Hart 1982; Townsend 1979; Gale and Hellwig 1985). In the typical case, the manager of a firm is argued to have objectives differing from the objectives and interests of the firm's shareholders and creditors. Therefore managers should be given incentives that would make them run the firm in the best interests of investors. Berle and Means's (1932) *The*

Modern Corporation and Private Property is usually referred to as the original study on the idea that managers pursue their own interests rather than the interests of shareholders. The agency theory developed by mainstream economics and popularly used by media, consultants and others raised questions such as 'is management delivering value?' or 'are managers acting for shareholders?' Froud et al., argue that this corporate governance approach is limited since '[it] sets up a mechanical universe where following or breaking rules of corporate governance has predictable results . . . [and] generally suppresses meso and macro analysis by constructing the economy as a bundle of corporations and the corporation as a bundle of investment projects' (2002a: 123–4).

Moreover, the agency theory is usually embedded in what would otherwise be a Walrasian general equilibrium model which has no contradictions or problems beyond principal–agent conflict. It trivializes the challenges faced by management – most of which have nothing to do with agency problems. Nevertheless, by the 1980s, 'the idea that the market for corporate control was a useful tool for enforcing managerial efficiency appeared in US Supreme Court decisions . . . and the Economic Report of the President for 1985 . . ., signaling that the financial model had graduated from minority view to orthodoxy' (Davis and Stout 1992: 609).

Below, I review four points of view that have critically engaged with the issue of corporate governance, starting with Lazonick and O'Sullivan, Froud et al. and other related research, then discussing various works written from a Regulation School perspective before discussing Stockhammer's (2004) attempt to investigate effects of these changes in corporate governance on capital accumulation. Finally, I discuss works that compare the corporate governance practices in other countries with those of the US.

'Downsize and Distribute'

Lazonick and O'Sullivan (2000), in their historical analysis of the rise of shareholder value as the principle of corporate governance in the US, observe a fundamental change in the corporate strategy: NFCs, until the 1970s, mostly adopted a strategy of retaining and reinvesting earnings with a view toward long-run profitability. However, since the early 1980s, this strategy has been transformed around downsizing the corporate labor force and distributing a higher share of earnings to shareholders. This strategic transformation, which has undermined the economic dynamism of the economy while simultaneously narrowing the social basis of prosperity, was the result of two developments: the worsening performance of corporations and the increased power of institutional investors along with the accompanying changes in corporate governance.[19]

Problems with the 'retain and reinvest' strategy started manifesting themselves strongly in the 1970s. Massive corporate expansion through internal growth as well as mergers and acquisitions during the 1960s was followed by poor performance in the 1970s since, Lazonick and O'Sullivan argue: 'corporations grew too big with too many divisions in too many different types of businesses' (2000: 15). The unstable macroeconomic environment of the 1970s together with the rise of new international competition, especially from Japan, exacerbated this problem. Hence, on the one side we see the negative effects of monopolization within the US and on the other side the pressures brought by rising global competition, bringing together the two strands of explanation on the causes of the accumulation crisis that I discussed above. It was during the 1970s, when the major manufacturing corporations in the US were struggling with 'excessive centralization' and innovative competition, that an approach to corporate governance known as 'agency theory' was being developed. At the same time 'the transfer of stockholding from individual households to institutions such as mutual funds, pension funds and life insurance companies made takeovers advocated by agency theorists possible and gave shareholders much more collective power to influence the yields and market values of the corporate stocks they held' (ibid.: 16).

Meanwhile, in the 1970s, a number of changes occurring in the financial sector were promoting the growth of equity-based institutional investing. Lazonick and O'Sullivan (2000) argue that:

> partly as a consequence of Wall Street's role in the buying and selling of companies during the conglomeration mania of the 1960s, from the early 1970s there was a shift in the focus of Wall Street financial firms from supporting long-term investment activities of corporations (mainly through bond issues) to generating fees and capital gains through trading in corporate and government securities. (p. 16)

Lazonick and O'Sullivan's framework provide an essential contribution to the debates around financialization and corporate governance in the way they analyse the financial sector. In the analysis they present, finance is not just some passive sphere into which investments are made but an active agent in the transformation of US corporate strategies especially in regards to distribution of corporate earnings to shareholders. They also point out the inherent fragility of this setup since it made the economy more dependent on the short-term decisions of financial markets. As will be seen in the discussion on the 'coupon pool capitalism' argument, Froud et al. provide a similar analysis. I will come back to a discussion on the significance of the dynamics of financial institutions in these frameworks after a brief review of Froud and her co-authors' various contributions to the debate.

'Coupon Pool Capitalism'

The shift to the 'downsize and distribute' paradigm of corporate govern-ance led to the rise of a 'coupon pool capitalism' as a distinctive feature of the era of financialization (Froud et al. 2002a). 'Coupon pool capitalism' differs from, what these authors call, 'productionism' as in the latter case the role of the capital market is only intermediation between savings of the households and the productionist firms whereas 'coupon pool is a new generic type where the pool of new and issued coupons becomes a regula-tor of firm and household behaviour and a regulator of macro economic trajectory' (ibid.: 126). Hence, 'coupon pool capitalism' is constituted when capital markets leave their traditional role of intermediation and begin regulating the behavior of firms and households (p. 126). Within this new configuration, the focus becomes shareholder value and value-based man-agement. Again, the emphasis is on more active financial markets and insti-tutions. Financial markets determine the requirement for returns on capital while they demand an increase in the proportion of corporate earnings distributed to financial markets.[20]

Froud et al. argue that an understanding of the economy through the concept of coupon pool capitalism does not necessarily predict outcomes (2002a: 130). Instead it highlights what needs to be investigated at a specific conjuncture. For example, in an economy with rising equity prices, house-holds enjoy a wealth effect depending on the size of their holdings while corporations themselves may be enticed toward financialization through dealing in speculative financial assets. The overall outcome in any case will depend on the size of the coupon pool, the scale of flows, norms of behav-ior and regulations (p. 131). As part of this framework, Feng et al. (2001) analyse the 'new economy.' They argue that the 'new economy' represented the variable, inconsistent and ongoing effects of financial market pressures on corporations. They show that between 1995 and 2000, new economy companies could use capital markets to finance their activities even in the absence of sufficient profitability. However, with the crash of technology stocks after 2000, these companies were required to produce profits in product markets. This has revealed the limits and fragility of the new economy fueled by financial expansion.

All in all, these analyses contribute to an understanding of how financialization via coupon pool capitalism makes the whole economy more sensitive and dependent on changes in financial markets, which could increase the potential instability of the economy. Of course, relating this framework to an analysis of how financial institutions and institutional investors operate would increase the explanatory power of the coupon pool capitalism approach. Lazonick and O'Sullivan, Froud et al. (2002a) and to a certain extent Feng et al. (2001) clearly see financial markets as active rather than passive agents. The literature on the operations of institutional investors, therefore, would be complementary to the discussions of the above reviewed authors on corporate governance. For example, D'Arista (1994b) points out that institutional investors tend to focus on factors that affect the price of outstanding stocks in the short-run instead of on the long-term objectives of the firm. This emphasis on short-term performance by institutional investors and corporate managers could result in less financing for research and development and hence undermine future growth performance (p. 265). As a matter of fact, this kind of behavior was long ago anticipated by Keynes, as Tobin argued:

> Keynes, himself an active and experienced market participant, despaired of 'investment based on genuine long-term expectation.' 'There is no clear evidence,' he said, 'that the investment policy, which is socially advantageous, coincides with that which is most profitable.' He noted that professionals, who bet on long-term fundamentals, while everyone else engages in short-term attempts 'to guess better than the crowd how the crowd will behave,' run greater risks. Not least of these is criticism for unconventional and rash investment behavior. Keynes' views would be confirmed today if he observed how professional portfolio managers seek safety from criticism in short-run performances that match their competitors and market indexes. (1984: 9)

Moreover, Parenteau (2005) makes a key observation when he notes that the short-termism of institutional investors finds its roots in the conditions of the industry as they are driven to increase their performances relative to each other: 'As competitive pressures built in the very profitable investment management business, this quickly evolved into a quarterly performance derby. . . . Despite the long-dated nature of the liabilities in corporate pension funds, consultants managed to herd investment managers into an absurdly short investing time horizon' (p. 123).

Furthermore, the enormous size of these institutional investor holdings curbs their ability to divest from firms with whose returns they are not satisfied. When the institutional investors are dissatisfied with the management, they cannot simply do the 'Wall Street Walk' as selling large numbers of shares could depress the share prices and hence harm themselves. Moreover, for the largest investors, the number of alternative investments is limited (Davis and Thompson 1994: 154). As a result, instead of exiting, these investors increasingly get involved in 'shareholder activism.' In short, critical discussions such as those of Lazonick and O'Sullivan as well as Froud et al. when taken with the literature on the dynamics of financial investors, especially institutional investors, enhance our understanding of the role of finance in the governance of NFCs.

'Regulation School' Perspectives

The impact of the financial sector on corporate governance, the question of financialization as part of a new accumulation regime and the role of finance in this regime has also led to some debates in the works of the Regulation School. Boyer (2000) and Aglietta (2000) attempt to explore the dynamics of the macroeconomy under the dominance of financial markets and the shareholder value movement and look at the effects of these on business decisions.[21]

Boyer (2000) uses the concept of 'finance-led growth' to describe what he calls a potentially new accumulation regime. A 'finance-led regime' would, according to Boyer, combine 'labor-market flexibility, price stability, developing high-tech sectors, as well as booming stock market and credit to sustain the rapid growth of consumption' (p. 116). However, this would only continue until the stock boom ends and the household borrowing hits its upper limit. In his model, financialization affects all institutional forms. While the privileging of shareholder value affects corporate governance, managers are also forced to review their management techniques, degree of specialization and the nature of capital–labor compromise. Furthermore, household behavior changes with a response to the wealth effects of financial markets. However, this point raises a question regarding the limits of wealth-led consumption and growth. The proportion of US families who hold stocks is much higher in the wealthier bracket of family income with $100 000 or more, whereas lower income families hold little if any stock (see, for example, Engen and Lehnert 2000). This raises questions regarding both the characteristics of consumption behavior in Boyer's model as well as the limits of such a wealth-led model.

According to Boyer (2000), within the finance-led growth model, Fordist capital–labor compromises are replaced by decentralization and individualization of labor contracts. Further, increased foreign competition replaces the oligopolistic competition of the previous era and challenges the viability of the earlier accumulation mode; a point also stressed by Crotty (2005). The prominence of the interests of creditors and shareholders creates a finance-based economy. However, in this analysis the new accumulation regime is fragile in the sense that its stability depends on inherently fragile financial structures. The governing force in this mode of accumulation is that of shareholder dominance.[22] The approach to financialization as a new regime of accumulation indeed helps to illuminate the fragility of capital accumulation under conditions of financialization.

Boyer provides an accurate description of the road from a Fordist accumulation regime to a finance-led one in the following long quote:

First, the monetarist counter-attack has meant the breaking-down of the Fordist capital–labor compromise and the beginning of a large decentralization and individualization of labor contracts and wages. Then the opening of the domestic market to foreign competition has induced erosion of the previous forms of oligopolistic competition, that in turn has challenged the viability of the previous wage–labor nexus. The emergence of large and long-lasting public deficits has developed broad and deep financial markets that have called for a liberalization of international saving. Therefore, during the subsequent period, financial deregulation and globalization have had the leading role in promoting the interests of creditors and of shareholders. The equity-based economy is the last and more recent stage of this process which took nearly a quarter of a century to affect the industrial, social and political structures of the US drastically. Consequently, it may be erroneous to attribute exclusively to finance all the interdependent and complementary transformations which took place in the hierarchy of institutional forms. The new economy is simultaneously more reactive to competition and product differentiation, based both on high tech and the extension of services to consumers, and, last but not necessarily least, governed by the impact of the shareholder's power and objectives. (2000: 143)

This model's viability has been discussed by Aglietta (2000), Aglietta and Breton (2001) and later by Boyer (2004). Aglietta and Breton draw attention to the negative implications of the rise of financialization for capital accumulation. They recognize that the types of financial systems promoted by financialization in turn have had effects on corporate strategies and hence the relations between capital accumulation and financial variables have changed in significant ways. They argue that net investment by NFCs is financed by retained earnings of the firms; hence an increase in financial payments could cause a decline in net investment, an argument similar to that of Duménil and Lévy.

Boyer (2004) argues that the limitations of the finance-led growth model became clear in the early 2000s. Operations undertaken in order to maximize shareholder value ended up reducing market share and profitability. An example of this is the merger between Chrysler and Daimler (p. 50). Moreover, 'the great liquidity of the US financial market led to a snowballing effect in the area of speculation' (p. 50). Hence, even though the shareholder value-driven accumulation regime may have been meant to provide dynamic growth by restructuring firms especially in the mature sectors, Boyer (2004) concludes that this did not materialize.

Financialization and Investment

Above, I pointed out that the consequences of financialization are potentially debatable. Stockhammer (2004) provides an attempt to empirically analyse the consequences of financialization for NFC investment. He starts with the observation that 'the past decades have witnessed a rise in investments in financial assets at the same time as a slowdown of accumulation of physical assets' (p. 719) in the US, UK, France and Germany. He argues that increasing 'financial activities [of NFCs] are interpreted as reflecting a shift in the firm's objectives and a rising influence of shareholder interests in the firm' (p. 721) and hence that the process of financialization is linked to changes in the internal power structure of the firm.

A central hypothesis of Stockhammer (2004) is that financialization has contributed to the slowdown in accumulation since the Golden Age. The consequence of this is that NFCs have become more rentier-like. This means, among other things, that they are less concerned with long-term growth and increasingly invest in financial markets instead of real capital accumulation. This happened through two institutional changes noted by Stockhammer:

> In the course of the 1970s, two institutional changes occurred which helped to align management's interests with shareholders' interests: the development of new financial instruments that allowed hostile take-overs and changes in the pay structure of managers. Among the former were tender offers and junk bonds (Baker and Smith 1998), among the latter were performance related pay schemes and stock options (Lazonick and O'Sullivan 2000). (2004: 726)

Stockhammer (2004) uses aggregate time series data from the US, UK, France and Germany to test this hypothesis and performs regressions for each country. After controlling for other variables such as the rate of capacity utilization, profit share and cost of capital, he finds that the rentier income of nonfinancial corporations – a variable used to proxy for financialization – is negatively correlated with investment for the US, although, the statistical results are neither very strong nor similar across countries. Hence he concludes '[o]ur tests can hardly be conclusive of our hypothesis that financialization has caused a reduction in accumulation rates, but they certainly provide strong initial support. The variable for financialization . . . fares as well as any standard variable in investment regressions (p. 736).

Stockhammer's empirical work demonstrates the possibility of a negative relationship between financialization and capital accumulation. He also points out the interrelatedness of two aspects of financialization, namely the increased involvement of NFCs in financial operations and the rising pressure of financial markets on NFCs to increase their short-term payments to the financial markets. Crotty as well as Duménil and Lévy also stress this point in their discussions of financialization and attempt to provide a framework to understand these changes. I come back to this issue in the next chapters when analysing the impact of financialization on capital accumulation.

International Comparisons

While financial liberalization and deregulation swept through the world, a shift towards US-style corporate governance also appeared in many countries. Debates on the financialization of the US economy and changes in corporate governance practices brought forward the question of whether these changes are specific to economies that have market-based financial systems as opposed to bank-based financial systems. Most of the literature has been concerned with comparing US-style stock-market-based systems with German and Japanese-style bank-based systems. These works made the argument that the stakeholder model of German and Japanese systems was superior for long-term growth to the US-style financial systems. The debates have been around the roles of financial systems in providing funding and key services to the corporate sector, as well as removing market imperfections. However, the effects of an increase in the size and power of the financial sector has not been discussed much in this literature. There are various case studies that show the changing corporate governance practices in other industrial countries, too (for example, Dore 2000, 2002; Morin 2000; Jürgens et al. 2000; Tainio 2003).

Dore (2000, 2002) analyses institutional and sociological aspects of financialization such as relations among corporations and financial institutions. His analysis compares and contrasts the American system with the Japanese and German systems. In terms of the rise of shareholder value, Dore (2000) points out that Japanese and German systems are different from the American system, as the rights of shareholders in these countries are circumscribed by the rights of stakeholders such as employees, customers, suppliers, subcontractors, creditors, local communities and so on (p. 10). Still, Dore argues that financialization and corporate governance changes are making inroads in Japan through internationalization of production, the increasing involvement of foreign investment funds in Japanese financial markets, as well as the ideological belief in the superiority of the US model (2002: 117).

Morin (2000) and Jürgens et al. (2000) observe similar developments in France and Germany, though they are not as extensive as in the US. According to their accounts, both France and Germany used to be network economies in which leading corporations are connected to each other in cross-shareholding. Committed shareholders (that is banks and other industrial companies) protect management from demands stemming from stock exchange pressures and the role of corporate management is to balance the interests and claims of different stakeholders in the corporation. However, according to Morin (2000), the French system increasingly resembles its American counterpart, as finance is gradually coming to dominate industrial capital. This domination, according to Morin, is happening through the opening of French share registers. Foreign investors have been allowed to enter French capital markets to the extent that they now own around 35 percent of French shares, the greater part of which is in the hands of American fund managers. Meanwhile, the cross-shareholdings system has been undermined from inside as French financial groups have begun to behave like value investors instead of playing their traditional role of patient shareholder. In Germany, by contrast, according to Jürgens et al. (2000), the industrial managers of giant companies were the ones who began pushing shareholder value as a target after a short and sharp recession at the beginning of the 1990s. In short, both the extent and the pace of transformation are different in these cases. While most of the old cross-shareholdings survive in France, they are in a process of losing their significance. However, shareholder value is a relatively more recent development in Germany where, despite the changes, the main elements of the system of corporate governance are still bank-based finance, industrial co-determination and productionist management orientations. Hence, Germany appears to be an economy in which 'shareholder value' has made some inroads but so far has not become the leading principle of corporate governance.

In more recent work, Tainio (2003) examines the financialization of top Finnish companies and the restructuring undertaken mainly to increase shareholder value and to enhance the companies' stock performance. He describes the financialization of four Finnish companies, pointing to the role of global investors in this process. Tainio argues that financialization in this case has its limits as the impossibility of indefinitely increasing market values favors an increase in managerial misconduct and crime.

In short, while there have been significant differences in financial markets and corporate governance practices across countries, it is possible to observe a convergence toward Anglo-American types of financial markets and corporate governance structures in many cases.

AN INITIAL FRAMEWORK TOWARDS UNDERSTANDING FINANCIALIZATION

The review of the literature up to this point reveals both different approaches to the issue of financialization and the limits of our knowledge on the issue. A few points regarding this literature are in order.

All works in the literature see the profitability crisis of the 1970s as one of the most significant causes of the transformations that followed. For the long-waves approach of Arrighi and others, this crisis is part of the structural long cycles of the capitalist system. Financial expansions always follow declines in the real economy. For some others, although structural conditions do play a great role, the political aspects of the drive towards financial market liberalization and deregulation is also of great importance. For example, Harvey, Duménil and Lévy and others emphasize that at the end of the 1970s and the beginning of the 1980s, the financial sector gained increased political power and was active in pushing for a more liberalized finance. The mainstream literature sees the late 1970s as a period during which corporate performance worsened mainly due to agency problems. Hence, solving the principal–agent problem would increase the efficiency of the corporation together with increasingly liberalized finance.

Most of the literature discusses the increased involvement of NFCs in financial investments and changing corporate governance structures separately. Crotty (2005) points out the interrelatedness of these two developments; while NFCs are pushed by financial markets to increase their financial payments and are faced with shortened planning horizons; this contributes to the drive towards more speculative and short-term investments by these corporations.

In addition, the literature is ambiguous in terms of the agency of the financial sector. For example, in Arrighi's framework finance is basically a passive space to which investments are directed after the overaccumulation crisis in the real sector. Harvey and Sweezy take a similar approach although they also tend to talk about the active agency of financial markets at certain points. Financial markets gain a more active role in corporate governance debates. Although part of the literature stresses the aggressive actions of financial agents, especially during the hostile takeover and of the shareholder value movements, at times finance turns passive and only responds to the needs and pressures of NFCs suffering from a declining profit rate. This is a constant tension in the literature. Finance has been a driving force behind the shift to neoliberal policies both in the US and in the 'developing' countries in the aftermath of loan pushing to the Latin American countries in the 1970s. In the US, finance has become a voracious innovator, regulation evader and stimulator of NFC actions such as mergers and acquisitions as well as financial investments. Following the Mexican default of 1982, the 'Washington Consensus' was created initially in order to save the US banks, a consensus later to be imposed on the rest of the world. For some authors who regard financialization as a component of the creation and reproduction of the global neoliberal regime, such as Harvey, this tension is apparent. While finance is seen as a sphere subject to profitability concerns of the NFCs, it is also seen as an active agent of change towards neoliberalism.

Indeed, as the earlier discussion of the historical context made clear, this is a key point in comparing the present with the previous era of finance capital at the turn of the 19th century. Recall that finance initially played a constructive role in the finance capital era of the late 19th and early 20th centuries. The banks in Morgan's Money Trust coordinated their own actions and the Money Trust brought order and growth out of the destructive competition of previous decades. The rise of massive inequality in this era and the role of deregulated financial markets in bringing about the Great Depression must not be overlooked, but neither should the positive contributions of economic coordination in ensuring smooth capital accumulation. The role of finance in the current era is quite different. Most of the literature on financialization emphasizes the destructive role of current financial markets. The giant financial institutions of this era provide no real sector coordination. Rather they feed destructive competition and undermine development strategies. However, even authors such as Panitch and Gindin, who attribute a positive role to finance, do not seem to undertake a comparison of similarities and differences between the present financialization era and the era of finance capital of the late 19th century.

There are certain questions that remain unanswered by the literature. The first regards the timing of the shift towards financialization. In most accounts, the end of the 1970s is considered to be the period during which the switch to increased investment in financial assets began. However, it is difficult to see this in the data. Indeed, the end of the 1970s and the early 1980s are the times when profitability in the financial sector was not high. Next is the question of the origin of financial profits and their relation to real sector profits. For example, Arrighi and others do not give a satisfying answer to the question of how financial profits can be high while real profits are low. Although the point that financial profits have been rising occupies a central position in many accounts, there is not much work done to uncover the sources of these increasing profits. It seems that several factors played a role in this since the early 1980s, including a rise in interest rates, increased debt during the 1980s hostile takeover movement, various debt explosions (US government, mortgages and household debt) and periods of speculative bubbles, especially the 1995–2000 stock market boom. In terms of the consequences of financialization, most of the literature reviewed focuses on negative impacts of financialization. A slowdown in the rate of accumulation, a depression of wages and an increase in potential fragility of the economy are among the consequences debated in the literature. Certain approaches, like Panitch and Gindin's, emphasize that financialization could be helpful to the capital accumulation process, an argument quite similar to that of the mainstream approaches. While Amin considers financialization as simply a mechanism to manage the ongoing troubles in the real economy, Arrighi anticipates a switch in world hegemony.

In light of the discussion of the historical context of financialization above in Chapter 3 and here on the debates around financialization, I present an outline to map the causes and consequences of financialization. Figure 4.2 is

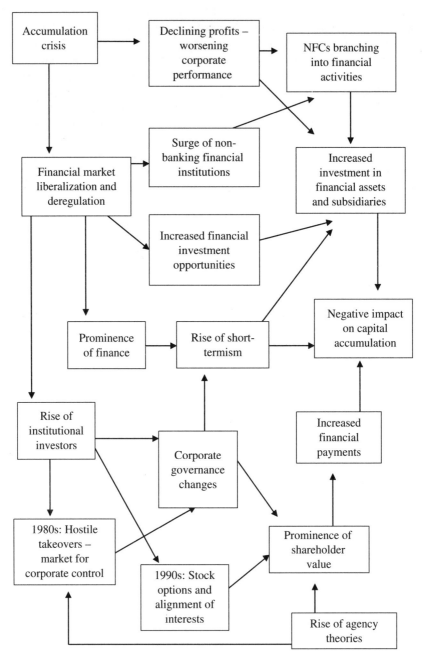

Figure 4.2   Causes and consequences of financialization of NFCs

one attempt to do this. It is not meant to be an all-comprehensive presentation but rather an outline of how different factors came together in forming today's financialized economy. The accumulation crisis of the 1970s created the conditions for financial market liberalization and deregulation which had significant impacts on the financialization tendency of the economy. The crisis was reflected in worsening of corporate performance and a decline in the profitability of the nonfinancial corporate sector. These problems in accumulation can be seen as one of the factors behind NFCs increasingly branching into financial activities. Financial market deregulation created an opening for the surge of non-banking financial institutions which has also become part of the cause behind the financialization of the NFCs. The liberalization and deregulation of financial markets also contributed to the growth of institutional investors. The rise of institutional investor holdings together with the creation of a market for corporate control via the hostile takeover movement of the 1980s and the following alignment of manager and shareholder interests via stock options, led to the prominence of the shareholder value movement in corporate governance. The spread of 'agency theories' would provide the theoretical basis and justification for these developments. As a result of this, NFCs, in an attempt to increase shareholder value in the short run and under pressure from the financial markets, increased their payments to the financial markets. Furthermore, financial market liberalization and deregulation in general increased financial investment opportunities, gave more power to the financial sector and created the conditions for NFCs to increase their investments in financial assets and finance subsidiaries. The resulting prominence of finance in economic decision making resulted in the replacement of long-term growth strategies with short-termist investments which played a role in allocation of a larger share of NFC funds to financial investments and financial subsidiaries. Increased financial investments by the NFCs and a rising cost of capital potentially had adverse effects on the rate of capital accumulation, among other outcomes. In the second part of this book I will discuss more in depth how these changes might have had negative impacts on capital accumulation through macro and firm-level analyses.

NOTES

1. I do not argue that there is no overlap among the topics discussed by the authors in each of these three categories. In every serious work on financialization, references are made to history, to the emerging global neoliberal system and to the effects of financialization on the structure and function of NFCs. Nevertheless, I believe that this tripartite segmentation adds to the analytical clarity of the discussion as well as allowing me to draw on the insights to be gained from these works.

2. Arrighi (1994) gives a detailed account of each of these cycles that are summarized in Table 4.1. See Arrighi (2005: 86–7) for a brief overview of these cycles.
3. For a succinct overview, see Bottomore (1983: 172–8).
4. For example, in the Dutch cycle mentioned above, intense interstate competition for mobile capital coupled with the escalation of the power struggle among them had created conditions for the Dutch financial expansion which temporarily inflated the wealth and power of the Dutch (Arrighi and Silver 1999: 52). By 1740 this was followed by increased British borrowing from the Dutch and by 1758 the Dutch held a third of Bank of England, English East India Company, South Sea stocks, and by 1762 the Dutch held a quarter of the English debt.
5. Arrighi and Silver (1999) also make similar arguments regarding financialization.
6. See Crotty (2000) for contradictions of the neoliberal era in regards to aggregate demand formation.
7. See Arrighi et al. (2003) for perspectives on the rise of China and how an adjustment would link to the resurgence of these economies.
8. In a recent review of this debate between Arrighi and Pollin, Blackburn remarks that:

> [t]he three possibilities they focused on were, firstly, where some capitalists were profiting at the expense of others; secondly, where capitalists as a whole are able to force a redistribution in their favour; and thirdly, where transactions had allowed capitalists to shift their resources from less to more profitable fields. However, we should also take into account two dimensions internal to finance itself: firstly, the cost of generating finance functions and products; and secondly, efficiency gains in anticipating risk. The financial revolution of the last two decades has registered large potential gains in dealing with risk; but most of this gain has been swallowed by the rising costs of financial intermediation, made possible by monopoly and asymmetric information resources, and generated by escalating marketing and trading expenditures as well as extravagant remuneration. (2006: 40–1)

9. In this analysis, it is not clear whether this measure captures NFC profits coming from financial subsidiaries.
10. See Crotty (2000) for a detailed exposition of these changes.
11 See pp. 138–43 for Harvey's (2003) discussion of 'overaccumulation' which finds its roots in Luxemburg's (1968) interpretation of Marx. For a more detailed discussion see Harvey (1982).
12. For a general discussion of economic problems of the neoliberal era, see Amin (2004).
13. Duménil and Lévy also attempt to differentiate long-term structural developments from elements that are specific to the financialized era as the following long quote lays out:

> It is first necessary to distinguish the long-term structural developments from elements specific to the neoliberal era. In the first category, it must be emphasized that in France, and to a lesser extent in the United States, the growth of financial portfolios reflects the relative development of corporations in relation to individual firms, and hence the multiplication of shares – a long-term historical movement. Moreover, in both countries a progressive institutionalization of investments is under way – financial portfolios are being transferred to institutional investors. This trend is also an old one, but was strengthened since 1980. Other transformations are specific to the 1980s and 1990s. First of all, we see an increase in activities by credit – households hold more credit (in the United States, households and firms simultaneously borrow and loan more than before). To that must be added in France, and certainly in the United States, the extraordinary growth in purchases and possession of stock by firms, denoting the establishment of a network of intercompany financial relations. This latter development is expressed by strong increases in financial revenues in relation to revenues linked to the main activity of firms. In this way, the traditional frontier between financial and nonfinancial firms tends to become blurred. (2004a: 118)

This argument gives rise to some important questions regarding financialization. Duménil and Lévy argue that part of the increase in the size of financial portfolios is reflected in the rise of publicly-held corporations as opposed to individual private firms. Duménil and Lévy see this as a historical trend both in the US and in France. This raises a twofold question: First, is the multiplication of shares a result of a historical movement from individual companies to publicly-held corporations, or do the increased availability of finance and the ease with which investors are able to obtain good terms cause private firms to go public and issue shares? Second, if the argument is correct, is it possible to measure what part of financialization is due to new corporations becoming publicly-held instead of remaining private? Intercompany relations are another interesting issue brought to the fore by Duménil and Lévy, though they do not detail their arguments. If proper data were available on the financial asset holdings of NFCs, it would be easier to evaluate their claims as well as identify intercompany relations in terms of their holdings of each other's stocks.

14. More recently Foster (2007) provides a discussion of the financialization process from the same perspective.

15. The political move towards financial market liberalization started in the 1970s, as I discussed briefly above. Two reports laid the grounds for financial liberalization. First, *1971 The Report of the President's Commission on Financial Structure and Regulation* which was the product of a group of industrialists and financiers convened by the president; and second *Financial Institutions and Nation's Economy Report* produced in 1975 (Isenberg 2000: 258). Significant changes came with various legislative steps from 1980 to 1994, of which the fundamental changes were as follows. The 1980 Depository Institutions Deregulation and Monetary Control Act modified the structure of interest rate ceilings, proposed the eventual elimination of Regulation Q and partially removing state-imposed usury ceilings. The 1982 Garn–St. Germain Depository Institutions Act authorized money market deposit accounts. The 1987 Competitive Equality Banking Act restricted the ability of non-banks to expand and created an incentive to convert themselves into a bank holding company. The 1989 Financial Institutions Reform, Recovery and Enforcement Act reorganized the regulatory apparatus for the savings and loan institutions. The 1994 Riegle–Neal Community Development and Financial Modernization Act allowed interstate branching.

16. I should also note that contrary to Arrighi's approach, Panitch and Gindin (2005) argue that the current era does not represent a new accumulation regime nor it is possible to talk about a shift in the world hegemony.

17. It is also interesting to note that one of the leading advocates of shareholder value, Jensen (2003) presents a disapproving evaluation of the last decade of financialization:

> In part the massive overvaluation of equity that occurred in the late 1990s and early 2000s was an understandable market mistake. Society often seems to overvalue what is new – in this case high-tech telecommunications, and Internet ventures. But this catastrophic overvaluation was also the result of misleading data from managers, large numbers of naïve investors, and breakdowns in the agency relationships within companies, in investment banks, and in audit and law firms many of whom knowingly contributed to the misinformation and manipulation that fed the overvaluation. (p. 14)

18. There are literally thousands of works on corporate governance. See Shleifer and Vishny (1997) and Allen and Gale (2000) for broad reviews of this literature and Gillan (2006) for an overview of recent developments.

19. For a discussion of the background of this argument see Lazonick and O'Sullivan (1997) and O'Sullivan (2000: chapter 4).

20. The concept of coupon pool capitalism is reminiscent of Engels's ([1877] 1976) remark in *Anti-Duhring* that '[t]he capitalist has no longer any social activity save the pocketing of revenues, the clipping of coupons and gambling on the Stock Exchange, where the different capitalists fleece each other of their capital' (pp. 359–60). However, Froud et al.

argue that the previous stage of capitalism before the rise of financialization was still more production oriented than today.

21. Grahl and Teague (2000) discuss the recent works of the Regulation School on financialization with a historical perspective on the Regulation approach.

22. Theorists from the 'social structures of accumulation' tradition also discuss the role of finance in contemporary capitalism and assess whether neoliberalism is a new social structure of accumulation. See for example Kotz (2003) and Wolfson (2003). In a more recent contribution Kotz argues that a financialized neoliberal regime can be considered as a new 'social structure of accumulation' within which the individual capitalists may prefer financial investments to productive investments:

> before the individual capitalist will plough profits back into new productive invest-ments, there must be an ability to make a reasonably determinate calculation of what the rate of profit on such investments will be, as well as the prospect that such a deter-minate rate of return will be acceptably high. The alternative is to hold the surplus value in another form, typically through some type of financial investment rather than real investment, while awaiting more favorable conditions for deciding to make a real investment. At times capitalists can make high rates of return through financial and speculative investments when the expected return to productive investment is either very uncertain or low. Such a situation would not impel them to transform institutions to produce a shift from speculative/financial investments to productive investments. (2007: 7)

PART II

Financialization and capital accumulation

5. Financial markets and NFCs: a theoretical discussion

Financialization, most broadly understood, refers to the increase in the size and significance of financial markets and financial institutions in the modern macroeconomy. There is certainly strong evidence to suggest that the relationship between the nonfinancial corporate sector and financial markets has become deeper and more complex in the process. We now know that over the last 20 years or so, NFCs in the US have been increasingly involved in investment in financial assets and financial subsidiaries and have derived an increasing share of their income from them. At the same time, there has been an increase in financial market pressures on NFCs. This has in part been due to changes in corporate governance, starting with the hostile takeover movement of the 1980s and proceeding to the so-called shareholder revolution of the 1990s (Lowenstein 2004). The same period has therefore also witnessed an increasing transfer of earnings from NFCs to financial markets in the forms of interest payments, dividend payments and stock buybacks. These developments reflect a change in the objectives of top management, an increasing propensity to short-termism in firm decision-making and/or increases in the cost of capital.

In the remainder of this study, I analyse changes that have taken place in the relationship between the nonfinancial corporate sector and financial markets and in particular, I ask the question of how financialization affects capital accumulation in the nonfinancial corporate sector. First, I discuss the changing nature of flows between financial markets and the NFCs and then move onto an analysis of the theoretical channels through which financialization would potentially have an impact on capital accumulation and then lay the ground for the empirical investigation that follows in the next chapters.

FINANCIAL MARKETS AND NFCs

The standard view in economic theory is that the financial sector provides necessary services to promote the investment activities of NFCs in productive assets. In very simple terms, the services provided by the financial sector offer certain advantages such as intermediation between lenders and borrowers, increased efficiency, reduced transaction costs, screening and monitoring of investments and risk management. According to the mainstream economic theory, purely financial transactions can take place due to market inefficiencies and incomplete markets. The role of purely financial transactions is then to correct for these problems, as Binswanger (1999) summarizes: 'Financial activities enhance the "real" efficiency of the economy or, which is the same thing, remove market imperfections' (p. 19).

If we look at the relationship between financial markets and the nonfinancial corporate sector, at the very basic level, leaving aside the question of efficiency, we see that NFCs acquire funding from financial markets in addition to their retained earnings to fund their activities. Funds can be raised through either equity issues or through different types of borrowing (commercial paper, corporate bonds and bank loans). When firms raise funds through issuing equity, they are expected to reward the holders of the stocks through dividend payments. When they use credit market instruments to acquire funding, they make interest payment commitments in addition to the promise of paying back the principal. Therefore dividend payments and interest payments are the two forms through which NFCs pay back to the financial markets for the capital raised. However, as Figure 2.14 showed, starting in the 1980s and more into the 1990s, the NFCs began to use stock buybacks as another way of making payments to financial markets. Although, as the name indicates, NFCs are mainly involved in nonfinancial economic activities, they can also use part of their resources to invest in financial assets. This results in NFCs receiving financial income in the forms of dividend income, interest income and capital gains. Hence, we observe a set of financial flows between financial markets and the NFCs, as summarized in Figure 5.1.

The largest and most important use of funds by the NFCs is the expenditures made to acquire capital goods for productive purposes. These capital expenditures can be financed with internal funds, equity issues or loans. Figure 5.2 shows the net funds raised in financial markets (including equity issues, debt securities and loans from banks and other financial institutions) by the NFCs as a percent of their capital expenditures. The net funds raised in financial markets show a drop in the early 1970s and another one in the late 1980s into the early 1990s. Although they briefly increased in the 1990s, they decline again starting in the early 2000s. This fact itself is important since at a time when the size of financial markets, transactions and instruments has been increasing, the role of financial markets in financing NFC operations has been in decline.

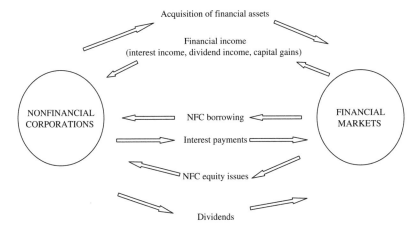

Figure 5.1   Financial markets and the nonfinancial corporate sector

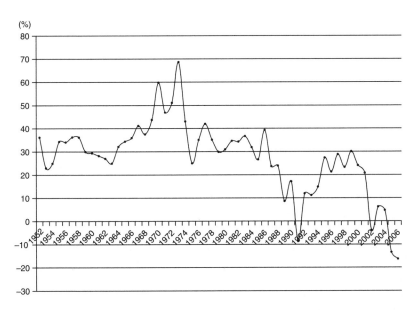

Source: FFA Table F.102.

*Figure 5.2   NFC net funds raised in the financial markets as a percent of
NFC capital expenditures, 1952–2006*

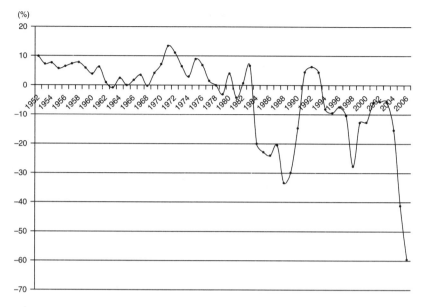

Source: FFA Table F.102.

Figure 5.3   *Net new equity issues as a percent of NFC capital*
            expenditures, 1952–2006

Issuing equities is another way to raise funds. Figure 5.3 shows net funds raised through equity issuance, this time as a percent of capital expenditures (recall that in Figure 2.14 we saw NFC stock buybacks as a percent of NFC gross value added). It is evident that the stock market has not historically been a major source of NFC funds. On a quarterly basis, its contribution never exceeds 18 percent of capital expenditures. On average its contribution has been below 10 percent, even in the 1952–1980 period before the increase in stock buybacks. However, there is a dramatic change in the relationship between the stock market and the NFCs starting in the early 1980s. Except for brief periods, in the post-1980 era the net equity issuance of the NFCs has been negative and often large. The NFCs have indeed been buying back their own stocks. The stock market has turned into an institution through which NFCs channel funds to financial markets, not the other way around.[1]

When we look at the sources of NFC funds, we see that corporate bonds have been a more important source and their contribution has increased in the post-1980 era. Figure 5.4 shows funds raised through corporate bonds as a percent of NFC capital expenditures. The amount of funds raised

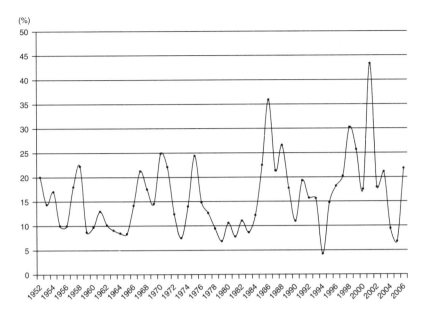

Source: FFA Table F.102.

*Figure 5.4   NFC funds raised through corporate bonds as a percent of
NFC capital expenditures, 1952–2006*

through corporate bonds by corporations varied a lot over time. In the
1952–1980 period these funds amounted to somewhere between 8 to 25
percent of the capital expenditures. In the financialization era the variation
in these funds increased, reaching almost 45 percent in 2001. The average
contribution of corporate bonds as a source of funding has been increasing despite a decline in the mid-1990s.

This brings us to the question of how then do NFCs fund their investments. Figure 5.5 shows the internal funds of the NFCs as a percent of their
capital expenditure. This figure demonstrates the importance of internal
funds for the funding of capital expenditures and other firm operations, a
point that was emphasized by Duménil and Lévy (2004a).

Turning to the other side of this relationship, let us remember the
changes in the payments made to financial markets for the funds raised
through these markets which I discussed briefly in Chapter 2. While NFCs
raise some funds through borrowing and equity issuance, in return they pay
out part of their earnings to financial markets in the forms of interest and
dividend payments. Figures 2.10 and 2.13 showed the trends in these expenditures. Interest payments to the financial markets increased fairly steadily

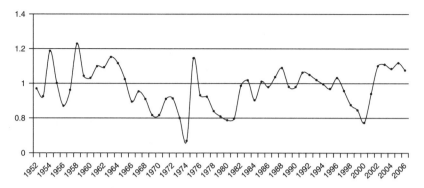

Source: FFA Table F.102.

*Figure 5.5   Ratio of NFC internal funds to NFC capital expenditures,
1952–2006*

up to the 1990s. After a brief decline at the beginning of the 1990s they
started to increase again, but have not reached the record levels of the end
of the 1980s. Dividend payments declined towards the end of the 1970s
alongside the decline in net equity issuance. They increased slowly in the
1980s and then with the stock market boom of the 1990s dividend payments as a percent of internal funds skyrocketed. All in all, payments made
to financial markets have been much higher in the financialization era compared with the earlier decades.

Consequently, we observe substantial changes in the flow of funds
between the financial and nonfinancial corporate sectors in that while the
amount of funds raised in the financial markets declined, payments to the
financial markets have increased. However, the changes are not only limited
to this side of the relationship. At the same time, we also see an increase in
investment in financial assets by the NFCs, as was shown in Figure 2.8. Of
course, NFCs derive income from these financial investments. Figure 2.10
showed the amount of this income, composed of interest and dividend
income, as a percent of NFC internal funds. While NFCs were increasingly
involved in investment in financial assets in the era of financialization,
deriving an increasing share of their income from financial sources and discharging higher amounts of payments to financial markets, the rate of
capital accumulation has been relatively low. Hence, the possibility of a link
between financialization and capital accumulation has attracted some
attention in the financialization literature. I now turn to the question of the
impact of financialization on the real capital accumulation process of the
NFCs.

FINANCIALIZATION AND CAPITAL ACCUMULATION

There are two main channels through which financialization could hamper investment in real capital assets. First, increased investment in financial assets can have a 'crowding out' effect on real investment. Total funds available to a firm can either be invested in real assets or used to acquire financial assets. When profit opportunities in financial markets are better than those in product markets, this creates an incentive to invest more in financial assets and less in real assets. There are two cases to consider. First, if we assume that external funds are limited because of quantitative constraints, because additional funds are only available at a higher cost, or because internal funds are 'safer' than external financing for the firm, then investing more in financial assets crowds out investment in real capital. Second, the pressure on firm management to increase returns in the short run can force them to choose financial investments, which provide more rapid returns, as opposed to real investments, which provide returns in the medium- to long-run. A counter argument might be that if the shift in investment spending from real to financial assets is only in the short run, this can add to the firm's funds in the long run and hence could potentially have a positive long-run impact on investment. If the firms are investing in financial assets when real investment is less profitable, earnings from financial investments could be used to fund real investment in the long run. I return to this question after I further discuss both channels and test which of these competing hypotheses is consistent with data.

A second channel through which financialization could undermine real investment is by means of pressure on NFCs to increase payments to financial markets in the form of dividends and stock buybacks by the firm.[2] Of course, if the evolution of financial markets and practices in the era of financialization lead to greater debt burdens on NFCs, interest payments will rise as well. The increase in the percent of managerial compensation based on stock options has increased NFC managers' incentive to keep stock prices high in the short run by paying high dividends and undertaking large stock buybacks. Simultaneously, the rise of institutional investors, who demand constantly rising stock prices, as well as the aftermath of the hostile takeover movement have pressured NFC managers to raise the payout ratio. NFC managers are thus motivated by both personal interest and financial market pressure to meet stockholders' expectations of higher payouts via dividends and stock buybacks (a shift in incentives) in the short run. Both the NFC objective function and its constraint set have changed. As a result, the percent of internal funds paid to financial markets each year has risen dramatically. This creates three distinct restraints on real investment. First, if internal funds are cheaper or safer than external financing, rising financial payments would decrease the funds available to finance real investment by reducing internal funds. Second, the time horizon of NFC management has dramatically shortened, hampering the funding of long-run investment projects, including research and development. Third, since the firm does not know how much it will cost to reacquire the financial capital it pays back to financial markets each year (that is, it has no idea what the cost of financing for ongoing long-term projects will be next year), uncertainty rises, making some projects with attractive expected gross long-term returns too risky to undertake. All three changes are aspects of the shift from 'patient' to 'impatient' investment financing.

Let me discuss each of these channels in more detail starting with the impact of increased financial investments and incomes, then turning to increased financial payments.

Expansion of Financial Investments and Incomes

The increase in the financial investments of NFCs and the resulting increase in their financial incomes have distinguished the last couple of decades of the US economy as shown above and as noted by, among others, Krippner (2005), Stockhammer (2004) and Crotty (2005). There has been a steady rise in the ratio of financial assets of NFCs to their real assets, which has been accompanied by a rise in their financial income. This significant rise in the financial investments and incomes of the NFCs, however, has not received much attention in the economics literature until very recently except in the works mentioned above. However, it has often been noted by the business press, along with cautions regarding the fragile character of financial earnings for the NFCs (see, for example, Eisinger (2004) and *Business Week* (2005)).

A potentially contradictory relationship between real and financial investment was identified by Tobin (1965). Before the literature on financialization and even before financialization took off in the 1980s and 1990s, Tobin noted that financial investment and real investment could be substitutes. Available funds can be invested in financial assets or real assets. He argued that in times when financial assets offer higher returns than real investment projects, more funds will be invested in financial capital and, as a result, fewer funds will be available for real investment. In other words, financial investment will crowd out real investment at least in the short run. He also noted that at the macro level, investment in financial assets cannot substitute for investment in real assets by a simple reallocation of funds into financial transactions, since no productive resources would be diverted from other uses by pure financial transactions at the aggregate level (Tobin 1997). However, Tobin did not elaborate further on these assertions.

Binswanger (1999) reasserts the crowding out argument for the current era of financialization and draws attention to the high rate of increase in financial investments relative to real investments by NFCs in the US. Crotty (2005) describes a similar process in which NFCs increased their financial investments and created or bought financial subsidiaries (or expanded the ones already in existence). He argues that this increase in financial investments was a response by NFCs to the low real sector profits and high costs of external funds faced during much of the 1980s and 1990s.

Stockhammer (2004) notes that higher financial profits together with changes in corporate governance led to a change in the priorities and incentives of corporate management. As a result of these institutional changes NFC management started adopting the preferences of financial markets which was reflected by a focus on short-term returns rather than long-term growth.[3] This change in managerial preferences had a negative effect on real investment, since NFC management now had fewer long-run growth-oriented priorities and instead chose to increase the financial investments of their corporations. Financialization pushed NFC management to act more like financial market players. Therefore, according to Stockhammer, the NFCs' shift towards financial investments can be interpreted as a shift away from the earlier managerial objectives of long-term growth through real capital accumulation which prevailed under the 'managerial firm' regime up through the 1970s, towards an adoption of institutional investors' interests in short-term stock price appreciation since the 1980s.

Crotty (2005) adds that since the NFC management's view of the firm has become increasingly dominated by the 'portfolio view of the firm,' short-termism has superseded long-term growth objectives. This portfolio view of the firm is summarized by Fligstein and Markowitz (1990) as the firm being seen as 'a bundle of assets to be deployed or redeployed depending on the short-run rates of returns that can be earned' (p. 187, quoted in Crotty 2002: 21).[4] This predominance of the portfolio view of the firm by management as well as by financial markets, together with hostile product market conditions that held the rate of profit on real assets down, created short-termism on the part of the NFC management that slowed down the rate of capital accumulation in the US compared with the earlier periods.

Increasing Financial Payout Ratios

Financialization has also been characterized by increased financial payout ratios in the form of interest payments, dividend payments and stock buybacks. Starting in the mid-1970s, total financial payments made by the NFCs have been increasing. Although it had its ups and downs, the post-1980 average of total financial payments has clearly been above that of the earlier era. Not only did interest payments and dividend payments increase, but firms also started buying back their own stocks and in effect making a payment to the financial markets. Lazonick and O'Sullivan (2000) label this phenomenon as a shift from a 'retain and reinvest' strategy to a 'downsize and distribute' strategy. As we have seen above, they argue that management became more focused on distributing the revenues of the corporation in ways that raised the company's stock price and increased the value of stock options. This is the result of institutional changes including the prioritizing of 'shareholder value' together with the rise of institutional investors, who focus on short-term stock price movements, the alignment of the interests of managers with those of shareholders through the use of stock options and the threat of takeover in the active markets for corporate control.[5]

Creating 'shareholder value' became more important with the rise of institutional investors such as mutual funds, pension funds and life insurance companies. Institutional investors have clearly become dominant shareholders in large US corporations and are responsible for about three-quarters of all stock trades (Crotty 2002: 23). We have already seen in Figure 3.2 that the share of corporate stocks held by institutional investors increased rapidly in the financialization era. This is important because, as Lazonick and O'Sullivan (2000) point out, the rise of institutional investors made the takeovers advocated by agency theorists possible, while giving shareholders increased power to induce the firm management to increase the yields and market values of the stocks they held. An OECD report presents this as a development in the efficiency of the financial markets:

> One of the most significant structural changes in the economies of OECD countries in the 1980s and 1990s has been the emergence of increasingly efficient markets in corporate control and an attendant rise in shareholders' capability to influence management of publicly held companies. In particular, owing to the expanded possibilities for investors to use the capital market to measure and compare corporate performance of corporations and to discipline corporate management, the commitment of management to producing shareholder value has become perceptibly stronger. (OECD 1998: 15)

The characteristics of competition among these institutional investors for asset management contracts force them to seek short-term capital gains or risk losing to competitors. This is the source of short-termism (see Parenteau 2005).

Duménil and Lévy (2004a) argue that the rate of capital accumulation in the nonfinancial sector closely follows that of the rate of retained profits (the rate of profit after payments of interest and dividends). Increased financial payouts in the forms of interest and dividend payments reduce retained profits and so should also diminish the rate of accumulation. Their theoretical argument is consistent with data for France and the US, where they observe that the rate of capital accumulation has slowed down while interest and dividend payments have risen.

Aglietta and Breton (2001) also discuss the rise of financial payouts. They study the relationship between developments in financial markets and the investment behavior of NFCs. Financialization creates an active market for corporate control, which forces firms to boost their share prices in the face of takeover threats. An active market for corporate control increases the influence of majority shareholders. In order to protect themselves and to please shareholders, corporations have to maintain a minimum return on equity, for which they have to distribute dividends or buy back their own stocks. As a result, not only is the share of firm funds devoted to real investment reduced, but if buybacks are financed by borrowing, then corporations may also increase their indebtedness and become more constrained by banks. Aglietta and Breton's (2001) theorization resembles that of Duménil and Lévy (2004a), with an added constraint that comes from increased indebtedness. They conclude that the market for corporate control can lead to a slowdown in growth by increasing the financial cost of capital, imposing constraints on management and increasing the indebtedness of the firm. As a result, increased financial payouts would have an indirect effect on investment through an increase in the total debt of the firm.

Moreover, Boyer (2000) points out that an increase in the return demanded by financial markets would have a negative effect on investment. Even though financialization can ease access to financial markets, it can also restrict investment by raising the cost of capital. Firms are best able to raise capital from the stock market when price–earning ratios are high, but in return they have to provide payments to the market in the form of dividends and stock buybacks or risk a stock price collapse. This is similar to Crotty's (1990) argument that payments to shareholders are a cost of autonomy for the management and hence these payments tend to constrain investment. For the management, dividend payments, like interest payments, can be considered as a cost of autonomy from financial market constituents. Therefore, the desired rate of firm growth must be balanced against the shareholders' demands, which could put a constraint on the growth objectives.

A counterargument could be that if financial markets are 'efficient,' firms should be able to raise funds to finance profitable investment opportunities. However, NFCs are in a position in which they first transfer a significant part of their earnings to the financial markets and then compete with all other borrowers to reacquire these funds. Recall that Froud et al. (2000) call this 'coupon pool capitalism,' where the earnings of corporations are returned to financial markets after which corporations compete to reacquire these funds. This process of discharging the earnings to the financial markets and then competing to reacquire them increases the degree of uncertainty and shortens the planning horizon for investment funding. Therefore, unlike the earlier era of 'retain and reinvest', managers now cannot be sure of the amount of these funds they will be able to reacquire and at what cost. This could especially hamper investments that have longer periods of gestation by creating uncertainty about the ability of the firm to finance the projects in the coming years. The pressure to provide high short-term returns to shareholders can shorten planning horizons, as the attempt to meet the short-term expectations of the financial markets, rather than investment in long-term growth of the firm, becomes the primary objective.

Increasing financial payout ratios have also been discussed extensively in the business and finance literature. However, the approach in this literature has been to focus on rather minor aspects of the phenomenon, such as the relationship between various indices of corporate governance, dividend payments and stock buybacks and corporate performance measured by return on equity.[6] This literature generally starts from the assumption of efficient financial markets. Consequently, the distribution of earnings to the financial markets at increasing rates cannot be seen as a factor that could hamper investment, since financial markets with full information would allocate firms the required amount of funds to undertake their optimum level of investment.

However, as stressed by Binswanger (1999), financial markets attract short-horizon speculative traders since these markets allow for sequential trading and react rapidly to any information which may influence expectations of market performance. Therefore, prices on financial markets tend to be volatile and enable profits (and losses) to be made within very short time periods. Managers of NFCs may be forced, or induced via stock options, to take the short horizon of financial markets as their guideline for decision-making. If financial markets undervalue long-term investments then managers will undervalue them too, as their activities are judged and rewarded by the performance of a company's stock price. This may harm the long-run performance of companies. As Crotty (2005) argues, there has been a shift in the financialization era from 'patient' financial markets to 'impatient' financial markets.[7] While the former regime emphasized the pursuit of long-term growth, the latter forces NFCs to pay an increasing share of their earnings to financial agents while also changing managerial incentives and shortening their planning horizons. Moreover, Jürgens et al. (2002) point out the interrelatedness of short-termism and the recent changes in corporate governance. They note that the shift towards a finance orientation and shareholder value could lead to lower levels of investment or outsourcing and downsizing if the financial targets can be met just by reducing investment (p. 66).

To sum up, I identify two channels through which financialization could have negative effects on investment in real assets. First, increased financial investments could have a negative effect by crowding out real investment and second, increased payments to financial markets can constrain real investment by depleting internal funds, shortening planning horizons and increasing uncertainty. In the next section, I develop an investment model that can be used empirically to test the relation between financialization and investment.

DETERMINANTS OF INVESTMENT AND FINANCIALIZATION

It is no surprise that the potential effects of financialization on investment have attracted much attention, as the 'pace and pattern of all business investment in fixed capital . . . are central to our understanding of economic activity' (Chirinko 1993: 1875). The growth of an economy ultimately depends on the accumulation of physical capital and the technology it embodies. However, it is not easy to empirically analyse investment as the 'estimation of investment functions is a tricky and difficult business and the best posture for any of us in that game is one of humility' (Eisner 1974: 101). Nevertheless, I will discuss the determinants of investment in order to specify a simple investment model that can account for the potential effects of financialization delineated in the previous section while controlling for other determinants of investment. After providing the theoretical motivation behind the model, I use it in the next chapters to empirically investigate the effects of the increased financial incomes and financial payout ratios of NFCs on their investment behavior.

There is a voluminous literature that attempts to explain the investment behavior of firms. The following discussion is based on the literature that attributes importance to both real and financial variables in the determination of investment behavior of firms (see, for example, Galbraith (1967); Eichner (1976); Lavoie (1992); Crotty (1990 and 1993); Crotty and Goldstein (1992)). The traditional literature, surveyed by Chirinko (1993) and Kopcke and Brauman (2001), focuses on a variety of issues that have importance in terms of investment. Five variables deserve attention in this regard. These are expected profitability, output or sales, the cost of capital and interest rates, cash flow or internal funds, and the debt ratio.

In what follows, I propose an investment model that includes both real and financial determinants of investment and introduces two financialization variables to account for the potential impacts of financialization on capital accumulation. The investment function is specified as:

$$I/K = f(\pi/K, S/K, D/K, P/K, \pi^F/K) \qquad (5.1)$$

where I is investment K is capital; π is profits; S is sales; D is long-term debt; P is financial payments; and π^F is financial profits; with the following expected signs:

$$(I/K)_{\pi/K} > 0,\ (I/K)_{S/K} > 0,\ (I/K)_{D/K} \gtrless 0,\ (I/K)_{P/K} < 0,\ (I/K)_{\pi^F/K} < 0,$$

Investment is expected to be positively related to the rate of profit and sales, and negatively related to two financialization variables, payments to the financial markets and financial profits. The sign of the debt variable will depend on managerial perceptions about the level of safe debt as discussed below. The profit and sales variables reflect both supply and demand conditions.[8] A discussion of these variables follows.

Profitability and Demand

On the real side, the growth opportunities of the firm depend on both demand and supply conditions. Profitability and demand are the two related constraints faced by the firm. The profitability objective is important as, *ceteris paribus*, firms will undertake investment projects that they expect to be profitable. As Kopcke and Brauman (2001) note '[a]ll models of investment recognize that businesses intend to profit from their investments. Yet, the models express this common theme in distinctive ways as they describe the influence of economic conditions on investors' perceptions of future profits and, in turn, on their demand for capital goods' (p. 8).

Within the literature, many contributions developed theories of capital accumulation that assign significance to profitability.[9] Expected profitability is a significant determinant of investment in neoclassical, q and options value models as well.[10] The framework I adopt here, however, is more in line with the literature which explicitly takes into account the fact that investors face 'true' uncertainty when they make investment decisions.[11] Under 'true' uncertainty, future profits and demand conditions cannot be known, so expectations about future conditions are in large part formed on the basis of past performance. Hence, past profitability becomes one of the major determinants of investment.[12] Moreover, if internal funds are preferred by management to external funds, past levels of profits could affect investment by determining the level of internal funds available for investment.

Investment is positively related to the expected future rate of profit on new capital investments. Given uncertainty about the future, it is reasonable to assume that the extrapolation of recent values of the profit rate on existing capital might be used as a proxy for the expected profit rate on new capital. But a problem with this is the fact that if the profit rate is affected by changes in the degree of capacity utilization, merely projecting past profit rates will not be a good predictor of investment. This is especially true if the degree of capacity utilization is likely to change in the future, or if the firm has been operating below full capacity in the recent past, in which case a high observed profit rate on capital does not imply a high expected profit rate on new capital. To take account of this problem, I use sales-to-capital ratio as a proxy for the degree of capacity utilization which has no good macro or micro measurement.[13]

Financial Payouts

Although I have argued above that we should expect a negative relationship between the financial payout variable and investment, this is not the only possible outcome. It could be argued that higher financial payments could mean higher future credibility by showing that the firm provides high returns to financial markets. A high financial payout ratio could signal profitability and solvency for the firm and also meet shareholders' liquidity preference. This can increase the firm's future access to finance and decrease the cost of finance by increasing the firm's creditworthiness. This would then imply an expectation that high financial payout ratios could be positively correlated with high investment. Nevertheless, an increase in the financial payout ratio in the above model may well affect investment in a negative way. The need to increase financial payout ratios indicates that the firm has to be careful in the short-run since failure to meet these financial payment obligations could result in loss of autonomy, a takeover threat and a fall in the value of stock options. Hence, increased financial payout ratios in the short run make it difficult to undertake investment projects that provide returns only in the long run and in the meantime require continuous financing. I will subject these competing theses to econometric analyses below.

Debt Ratios

Debt-to-equity or debt-to-capital ratios have been used in investment models with the idea that high levels of debt indicate financial fragility which would have negative effects on the investment behavior of the firms.

As the debt ratio increases, managers and shareholders incur a growing risk of losing control of their firms. The overall indebtedness of the firm reflects the long-run financial safety of the firm as higher levels of debt increase the fragility of the firm's balance sheet. Hence, debt-to-equity or debt-to-capital indices measure a firm's long-term financial fragility. The relation between investment and debt should depend on the level of debt perceived as safe by the firm's management and by financial markets. If the level of debt is perceived to be above the safe level, then increases in total debt would have a negative effect on investment. Conversely, if the level of debt is below the safe level, then it will either have no effect or a positive effect through an increase in the funds available for the firm.[14] The level of safe debt may vary with the size of the firm as well as with attitudes to firm indebtedness. Such attitudes may change over time.[15] In the height of the hostile takeover movement of the 1980s, high debt was considered to be good for the firm because it forced managers to be efficient, thus minimizing the principal–agent problem, while it protected the firm from hostile takeovers. Moreover, debt financing of investment creates at least a short-run correlation between debt and investment.

Nonetheless, high leverage can also constitute a threat to the autonomy of the firm management. Increasing debt indicates higher cash flow commitments by the firm to its creditors. If the future income of the firm turns out to be insufficient to meet these commitments, the management then faces the risk of losing its decision-making autonomy as well as of the firm going bankrupt.[16]

Short-termism and Financial Profits

The expectation of a negative coefficient for the financial profit variable developed above is potentially contentious. For one thing, this expectation is in contrast with the financing constraint hypothesis. According to the financing constraint hypothesis, any income, whether from financial or real sources, would contribute to the internal funds of the firm and hence its effect on investment should be positive.[17] If in the future, the profit rate on financial assets falls below the profit rate on real assets, firms may use their income from current financial operations to finance their future real investment projects. In this case, past financial income can be positively correlated with the level of current capital expenditures.

I will come back to these arguments while discussing the empirical findings. However, two considerations should be noted. First, it is generally considered to be the case that smaller firms are more likely to be financially constrained than larger firms. Therefore, a positive effect of financial income on real investment for smaller firms can in principle be identified through the use of firm-level data. Second, even though financial income could be treated as any other income, there is no guarantee that it would be used to finance real investment. Given the increased pressure on the firms to discharge their earnings to the financial markets, financial income might be recycled back to financial markets or used to purchase yet more financial assets.

THE EMPIRICAL AGENDA

Up to this point, I have developed a theoretical framework to discuss and empirically analyse the implications of financialization for the NFC capital accumulation process. Increased financial investments and incomes as well as increased payments to the financial markets could have negative impacts on NFC investment through the channels discussed above. An investment model that accounts for both real and financial determinants of investment has been introduced to be used in econometric analysis of the relationship between financialization and real investment. Using this model, I will test the effects of financialization on real investment, first with aggregate time-series data for the US and then with firm-level data. Macro data help us to look beyond the specific details of different industries' and/or type of firms' investment behavior and to isolate fundamental relations that govern capital accumulation. Firm-level data help to identify the reaction of different industries and firms to changes in these relations. In the next chapter, I start with aggregate time-series analysis and then turn to firm-level analysis in Chapter 7.

NOTES

1. In their detailed research on the European auto industry, Jürgens et al. (2002) find that none of the four biggest European auto companies (Fiat, PSA, Renault, VWAG) 'needed the stock market for its operational activities, including major investment in new facilities and new product programmes' (p. 78). This reiterates the point made by Figure 5.3, in the European context.
2. Including stock buybacks in financial payments is important. For many major NFCs, stock buybacks 'have now become a systematic feature of the way in which they allocate revenues and a critically important one in terms of the money involved' (Lazonick and O'Sullivan 2000: 23). Moreover, Grullon and Michaely (2002) show that stock buybacks 'have not only become an important form of payout for US corporations, but also that firms finance [stock buybacks] with funds that otherwise would have been used to increase dividends' (p. 1649).
3. This short-termism has recently attracted widespread attention in the business press. The *Financial Times* reports that 'a consensus is forming among chief executives, regulators and analysts against the quarterly ritual that encourages management to pursue narrow, short-term targets at the expense of more sustainable growth' ('Opposition grows to earnings forecasts' by Dan Roberts, 13 March 2006, p. 1).

4. According to Fligstein and Markowitz (1990) '[t]he normative acceptance of hostile takeovers in the 1980s reflected the more general triumph of this view of the corporation'.
5. This literature and its critiques were reviewed in Chapter 4. Main works in this literature are: Jensen and Meckling (1976); Ross (1977); Grossman and Hart (1982); Townsend (1979); Gale and Hellwig (1985); and Baker and Smith (1988).
6. Bhagat and Jefferis (2002) provide a concise overview of the important contributions in this literature. See Allen and Michaely (1995) and Lease et al. (2000) for comprehensive reviews of the literature on dividends. Baker et al. (2002a and 2002b) review the literature on stock buybacks.
7. Literature on institutional investors demonstrate that equity markets dominated by them tend to undervalue firms with good earnings prospects in the long term but low current profitability. This in turn is held to discourage long-term investment or investment in research and development as opposed to distribution of dividends (Davis and Steil 2001: 323–5).
8. It is a standard assumption that investment is determined by the cost of capital, which essentially includes the price of investment goods, expected rates of return and the tax impacts as stressed in a classical article by Jorgenson (1971). Jorgenson's strong findings in favor of cost of capital as a primary determinant of investment is not supported by more recent works, including Fazzari et al. (1988).
9. See, for example, Marglin and Bhaduri (1990), Bhaskar and Glyn (1995). These studies all consider expected profitability to be one of the most significant determinants of investment.
10. See Kopcke and Brauman (2001) for a review of these usages.
11. The expectation formation under 'true' uncertainty is different from that in the neoclassical theory which uses a subjective probability function. Firm management form their expectations based not on a probability function but instead on 'institutional, social and psychological' conditions. See Crotty and Goldstein (1992) for a discussion of the implications of uncertainty for firm investment behavior.
12. As noted by many, including early studies done by Kuh and Meyer (1955) and Minsky (1975), current and past profits could serve as indicators of future profitability.
13. Moreover, Kuh and Meyer (1955) and Eisner (1958 and 1960) developed earlier versions of accelerator models in which permanent increases in output/sales induce an increase in capital stock. Later studies such as Fazzari (1993) and Chirinko (1993) also account for a sales effect.
14. Another channel through which high debt would have an effect is put forward by Duesenberry (1958) who emphasizes the opportunity cost of debt:

    As debt rises relative to earnings, the risk premium required to cover the leverage of debt service on earnings fluctuations will increase. The opportunity cost of not repaying the debt will therefore increase. That opportunity cost increases the return required to justify investing in physical assets whether the investment involves taking an additional debt or failing to repay existing debt. (p. 94)

15. For Minsky (1975 and 1986), debt affects investment through the management's perception of the extent of financial fragility or robustness of the firm in the long run. See also Crotty and Goldstein (1992: 201) for a similar point of view. Ideally, one would like to be able to measure the difference between the current level of indebtedness and the level the management considers safe in the long term. Since such a measure is not available in the dataset I use, I leave the expected sign on the coefficient of the debt level indeterminate at the moment.
16. See Crotty and Goldstein (1992) for a thorough discussion on the formation of perceptions on safe debt levels.
17. See, for example, Fazzari et al. (1988), Gertler and Gilchrist (1994) and Ndikumana (1999), for details and applications of the financing constraint hypothesis.

6. Financialization and investment: aggregate analysis

Financialization can have two potential negative impacts on capital accumulation, as discussed in the previous chapter. First, increased financial investment and financial profit opportunities can crowd out real investment by creating managerial short-termism and directing funds away from real investment. Second, increased financial payments can decrease real investment by decreasing the quantity of available funds for real investment, shortening the planning horizons of firm management and increasing uncertainty. These two potential negative effects are taken into account in the investment model described above. In this chapter, I econometrically test the effects of financial profits and financial payments of NFCs on their real investment, using aggregate time-series data for US NFCs. I find that the role played by these two variables is empirically supported by the econometric analysis, although statistical significance of the parameters is low in some cases. Nevertheless, the results provide initial support for a negative relationship between financialization and real investment.

This chapter is organized as follows. In the next section, I present the statistical specification to be tested and discuss the properties of the data. I turn to econometric issues in the second section and present regression results in the third one. Finally, the last section provides an evaluation of the results and lays the ground for the firm-level analysis to follow in the next chapter.

STATISTICAL SPECIFICATION AND DATA

The discussion of the determinants of investment in fixed assets in Chapter 5 considered traditional variables such as rate of profit, sales and long-term debt and introduced financialization variables into the equation. Following that discussion, the investment function to be estimated in this section takes the following form:

$$I = \alpha_0 + \alpha_1 \pi + \alpha_2 GVA + \alpha_3 D + \alpha_4 \pi^F + \alpha_5 P + \gamma \qquad (6.1)$$

where I is investment in fixed assets, π is profits, GVA is the gross value added of NFCs, D is total debt of NFCs, π^F is the sum of interest income and dividend income for NFCs, and P is the sum of interest payments, dividend payments and stock buybacks by NFCs. In this specification, the π and GVA variables account for the effects of expected profitability and capacity utilization on investment, as discussed in the previous chapter. D measures the impact of debt on investment. The two financialization variables introduced, P and π^F, account for the effects of financialization. The relationship between these variables and the rate of investment was discussed in the previous chapter. Recall that the coefficients of these variables are expected to have the following signs:

$$\alpha_1 > 0,\ \alpha_2 > 0,\ \alpha_3 \gtreqless 0,\ \alpha_4 < 0,\ \alpha_5 < 0$$

The real variables, the rate of profit and output, are expected to have a positive impact on investment while the financialization variables are expected to have a negative relationship with investment. Debt could have a positive or a negative relationship with investment depending on conventions about the level of safe debt, as discussed above. For example, if recent experience has been that outstanding debt was easily serviced then firms might tend to increase their debt in order to finance more investment. In the opposite situation, conventional safe debt ratios could decline in which case the relationship between debt and investment could turn negative.

The equation specified abstracts from issues of levels versus rates and the lag structures imposed. In the empirical tests, these variables will be expressed as ratios to the beginning of period capital stock, K, and lagged values of the explanatory variables will be used:

$$(I/K)_t = \alpha_0 + \alpha_1(\pi/K)_{t-1} + \alpha_2(GVA/K)_{t-1} + \alpha_3(D/K)_{t-1}$$
$$+\ \alpha_4(\pi^F/K)_{t-1} + \alpha_5(P/K)_{t-1} + \gamma \qquad (6.2)$$

Using lagged values of explanatory variables in the investment equation is important because of the time lag between the investment decision and capital expenditures and their role in expectation formation. Moreover, lagged explanatory variables help avoid problems of simultaneity and reverse causation.

Summary statistics for the variables and definitions and sources of these data items are reported in Appendix A, Tables 6A.1 and 6A.2, respectively. Annual frequency data will be used in estimations. There are two reasons for this. The practical reason is that key financialization variables are only available on an annual basis. National Income and Product Accounts

(NIPA) report data on interest income and dividend income on an annual basis. On the theoretical side, investment in fixed assets is thought to be a long-term decision; therefore it is more likely that annual data would reflect the determinants of real investment better than higher frequency data. Investment and capital stock items are deflated by the price index for capital goods in order to obtain real values. All other variables are deflated by the price index for gross domestic product. The sample period is 1961–2004. This is the period for which all data items are available after taking necessary lags. While most data items are available starting from 1952, interest income and dividend income variables only become available after 1958. The period for estimations though, starts from 1961 as observations are lost due to taking lags and differences, as discussed below. In order to take into account potential nonlinearities the equation will be presented in natural logarithms. Hence the equation to be estimated takes the following form:

$$\ln(I/K)_t = \alpha_0 + \alpha_1 \ln(\pi/K)_{t-1} + \alpha_2 \ln(GVA/K)_{t-1} + \alpha_3 \ln(D/K)_{t-1}$$
$$+ \alpha_4 \ln(\pi^F/K)_{t-1} + \alpha_5 \ln(P/K)_{t-1} + \gamma \qquad (6.3)$$

ECONOMETRIC ISSUES

Table 6A.3 in Appendix A presents the correlation matrix between regression variables. This table shows that there is potentially a high degree of correlation among some explanatory variables. The high degree of correlation between the financial profits variable and the financial income variable might make it hard to distinguish the effects of these variables from one another. Moreover, time-series estimates could potentially suffer from problems such as heteroscedasticity, unit roots and autocorrelation. Since variables in the above equations are expressed as ratios to the beginning of period capital stock, heteroscedasticity problems are likely to be avoided.

A significant issue with time-series analysis is the existence of unit roots. Many time-series data violate the assumption of stationarity. Ideally, one would like to have stationary time series – series generated through a stochastic process – in order to econometrically analyse the series. Stationary series would have a mean to which there would be a tendency for the series to return. Moreover, stationary series would have a finite variance and shocks to the series would be transitory. For non-stationary series, the variance is infinite, shocks are permanent and the autocorrelation of the series tends to one. Figures 6B.1 to 6B.6, presented in Appendix B, provide time-series plots of the variables in this equation, natural logarithms of rate of investment, rate of profits, gross value added, debt ratio, financial profits and financial payments, respectively. These plots suggest that most data series used here are non-stationary. I apply unit root tests. First, I use the conventional augmented Dickey–Fuller (ADF) unit root tests. However, since the ADF test is thought to have low power to reject the null hypothesis of a unit root, especially in shorter time series, I employ two additional unit roots tests; DF–GLS and Phillips–Perron tests.[1]

Table 6A.4 presents the results of the ADF tests. We observe that for all variables we fail to reject the null hypothesis that the variable contains a unit root. Indeed, we are only able to reject the null hypothesis for the dependent variable at the 5 percent statistical significance level. Next, in Table 6A.5, I present the results of the DF–GLS unit root tests. This test performs a modified Dickey–Fuller test for a unit root after transforming the series by a generalized least-squares regression (Elliott et al. 1996; Stock and Watson 2003: 549–52). DF–GLS unit root tests also indicate the presence of a unit root in the variables. Finally, results of Phillips–Perron unit root tests are presented in Table 6A.6. This alternative test for unit roots has the same null hypothesis as the earlier ones (Hamilton 1994: Chapter 17). Results of this test also fail to reject the null hypothesis that variables contain a unit root.

Standard practice in time-series econometrics is to take first differences of the series in order to make them stationary. In the next step, I take first differences of the variables and apply the same unit root tests in order to see whether the differenced series are now stationary. Tables 6A.7, 6A.8 and 6A.9 show that taking first differences of the series make them stationary. Therefore, I use the first differenced series in the regression analysis.

The differenced equation to be estimated takes the following form after variables were first-differenced in order to make them stationary:

$$\Delta\ln(I/K)_t = \alpha_0 + \alpha_1\Delta\ln(\pi/K)_{t-1} + \alpha_2\Delta\ln(GVA/K)_{t-1}$$
$$+ \alpha_3\Delta\ln(D/K)_{t-1} + \alpha_4\Delta\ln(\pi^F/K)_{t-1}$$
$$+ \alpha_5\Delta\ln(P/K)_{t-1} + \gamma \qquad (6.4)$$

where Δ stands for the difference operator. In the next section, I provide estimation results for this equation using time-series methods.

REGRESSION RESULTS

Equation 6.4 is estimated through ordinary least squares and the results are presented in Table 6.1. Column I shows results for the original equation. The rate of profit variable has the expected positive coefficient and is

Table 6.1   Aggregate regression results with differenced variables

Dependent variable: rate of investment	I	II	III	IV
Rate of investment in the previous year		0.172		
		(0.218)		
Gross value added	0.231	0.251		0.162
	(0.377)	(0.38)		(0.35)
Rate of profit	0.389***	0.442***	0.419***	0.408***
	(0.112)	(0.132)	(0.1)	(0.105)
Financial payments	−0.326**	−0.305*	−0.298*	−0.308*
	(0.158)	(0.161)	(0.15)	(0.152)
Financial profits	−0.274	−0.205	−0.253	−0.248
	(0.211)	(0.229)	(0.206)	(0.202)
Debt	0.257	0.323	0.151	
	(0.496)	(0.506)	(0.461)	
R-squared	0.39	0.41	0.39	0.39
Adjusted R-squared	0.32	0.31	0.31	0.33
Breusch–Pagan/Cook Weisberg test for heteroscedasticity H_0: constant variance	1.73	0.54	1.81	2.39
Ramsey test H_0: model has no omitted variables	1.01	3.13	1.18	0.87
Breusch–Godfrey LM test for autocorrelation H_0: no serial correlation	0.673	0.697	0.41	0.65
Durbin's alternative test for autocorrelation H_0: no serial correlation	0.575	0.724	0.35	0.57

Notes:
Standard errors in parentheses.
* indicates significance at 10 percent, ** significance at 5 percent and *** significance at 1 percent.

statistically significant at the 1 percent level. While the gross value added variable has the anticipated positive sign and has a large coefficient, it does not have statistical significance at the traditional 1, 5 and 10 percent levels. The debt to capital variable has a positive sign, although it also lacks statistical significance at the traditional levels. Finally, both financialization variables introduced have the expected signs. Both the financial payout and the financial profits variables enter the equation with large negative coefficients. The financial profits variable is statistically significant at the 5 percent level.

Post-regression tests show that this specification is free from the usual time-series problems, such as heteroscedasticity and autocorrelation. R-squares of the results are around 0.40, which is not a low level for differenced regression results. Furthermore, post-estimation tests for potential problems are reported on the lower block of Table 6.1. The heteroscedasticity test, omitted variables test and autocorrelation tests performed do not show any of these problems.

In order to test the robustness of these results, I present three more equations. In Column II a lagged value of the dependent variable is introduced into the equation;[2] in Column III the estimation is performed without the gross value-added variable and in the last column the equation is tested without the debt variable. In all three estimations the rate of profit variable has a positive and statistically significant coefficient. Signs for other variables are not sensitive to these different specifications. The financial profits variable always has the negative sign predicted by the theoretical framework, although its statistical significance declines slightly with alternative specifications. The financial payout variable is also robust to these alternative specifications and always has a negative coefficient.

Thus, the macro econometrics results support the hypothesis that financialization constrains capital accumulation. While it was acknowledged that there could be positive effects of financial profits and financial payouts on investment, the econometric tests suggest that such positive effects, if they exist, were dominated by negative effects. Though the coefficients on financial profits are not statistically significant at the 10 percent level, the fact that they are negative in all four forms of the regression suggest that the negative relationship may be more than random.

FROM MACRO TO FIRM-LEVEL ANALYSIS

So far I investigated the potential negative impacts of financialization on NFC investment through an econometric analysis of the aggregate US data. After a discussion of the time-series properties of the data, regression analysis was performed with differenced time series. The econometric tests gave modest support to the hypothesis that financialization could hamper real investment. Effects of financial profits and financial payments variables on investment are found to be negative and are robust to alternative specifications.

However, as argued in the theoretical literature, it is likely that financialization had different impacts on firms of different sizes and industries. Thus, the macro regressions may give misleading results due to the aggregation of heterogeneous firms. Therefore, in the next chapter, I turn to a firm-level analysis of the effects of financialization on investment. Firm-level data not only improve the statistical precision of the tests thanks to the availability of a larger sample size, but also make it possible to analyse the differential impacts of financialization on capital accumulation for firms with different characteristics. I postpone the discussion of larger implications of these findings here to the end of the firm-level analysis.

NOTES

1. This latter test has also been criticized for its weak power. I provide the results of the test in Appendix A to show that the finding of a unit root in series is robust across different unit root tests.
2. As I discuss in detail in the next chapter, including a lagged value of the rate of investment among the independent variables helps to control for dynamic effects such as gestation in time and inertia.

APPENDIX 6.A: PROPERTIES OF THE DATA SET AND TEST STATISTICS

Table 6A.1   Summary statistics

Variable	Number of observations	Mean	Standard deviation	Minimum	Maximum
I/K	44	0.086	0.014	0.062	0.114
π/K	44	0.071	0.025	0.033	0.125
GVA/K	44	0.282	0.230	0.030	0.692
D/K	44	0.422	0.063	0.326	0.516
π^F/K	44	0.023	0.010	0.001	0.041
P/K	44	0.084	0.021	0.053	0.128

Table 6A.2   Variable definitions and sources

Variable	Description	Source
Investment	Capital expenditures	Flow of Funds Accounts Table F.102
Capital stock	Total nonresidential fixed assets	Flow of Funds Accounts Table B.102
Profits	Profits before tax	Flow of Funds Accounts Table F.102
Gross value added	Gross value added of NFCs	BEA NIPA Table 1.14
Debt	Total debt	Flow of Funds Accounts Table B.102
Financial profits	Interest received + Dividends received	BEA NIPA Table 7.10 BEA NIPA Table 7.10
Financial payments	Interest paid + Dividends paid + Stock buybacks	BEA NIPA Table 7.10 BEA NIPA Table 7.10 Flow of Funds Accounts Table F.102
Price indices	Price index for GDP Price index for capital goods	BEA NIPA Table 1.14 BEA NIPA Table 1.14

Table 6A.3 Correlation matrix

	I/K	π/K	GVA/K	D/K	π^F/K	P/K
I/K	1					
π/K	0.23	1				
GVA/K	0.31	−0.66	1			
D/K	0.36	−0.48	0.86	1		
π^F/K	0.27	−0.72	0.91	0.74	1	
P/K	0.29	−0.66	0.80	0.71	0.90	1

Table 6A.4 Augmented Dickey–Fuller unit root tests

		Test statistics	1% critical	5% critical	10% critical
$\ln(I/K)$	$Z(t)$	−3.097	−3.628	−2.95	−2.608
$\ln(\pi/K)$	$Z(t)$	−1.633	−3.628	−2.95	−2.608
$\ln(GVA/K)$	$Z(t)$	−2.102	−3.628	−2.95	−2.608
$\ln(D/K)$	$Z(t)$	−0.994	−3.628	−2.95	−2.608
$\ln(\pi^F/K)$	$Z(t)$	−1.803	−3.628	−2.95	−2.608
$\ln(P/K)$	$Z(t)$	−1.274	−3.628	−2.95	−2.608

Notes:
H_0: Variable contains a unit root.
H_1: Variable was generated by a stationary process.

Table 6A.5   *DF–GLS unit root test*

Lags	DF–GLS test statistic	1% critical value	5% critical value	10% critical value
ln(I/K)				
9	−1.426	−3.77	−2.712	−2.398
8	−2.299	−3.77	−2.768	−2.464
7	−2.493	−3.77	−2.836	−2.537
6	−1.998	−3.77	−2.912	−2.615
5	−2.459	−3.77	−2.993	−2.695
4	−2.07	−3.77	−3.074	−2.773
3	−2.171	−3.77	−3.152	−2.846
2	−2.268	−3.77	−3.222	−2.912
1	−2.75	−3.77	−3.283	−2.968
ln(π/K)				
9	−1.349	−3.77	−2.712	−2.398
8	−1.342	−3.77	−2.768	−2.464
7	−1.842	−3.77	−2.836	−2.537
6	−1.766	−3.77	−2.912	−2.615
5	−2.264	−3.77	−2.993	−2.695
4	−2.156	−3.77	−3.074	−2.773
3	−2.23	−3.77	−3.152	−2.846
2	−2.207	−3.77	−3.222	−2.912
1	−2.893	−3.77	−3.283	−2.968
ln(GVA/K)				
9	−1.528	−3.77	−2.712	−2.398
8	−1.643	−3.77	−2.768	−2.464
7	−1.619	−3.77	−2.836	−2.537
6	−1.674	−3.77	−2.912	−2.615
5	−2.493	−3.77	−2.993	−2.695
4	−2.362	−3.77	−3.074	−2.773
3	−2.232	−3.77	−3.152	−2.846
2	−1.705	−3.77	−3.222	−2.912
1	−1.211	−3.77	−3.283	−2.968
ln(D/K)				
9	−2.107	−3.77	−2.712	−2.398
8	−2.438	−3.77	−2.768	−2.464
7	−2.347	−3.77	−2.836	−2.537
6	−2.807	−3.77	−2.912	−2.615
5	−2.569	−3.77	−2.993	−2.695
4	−2.453	−3.77	−3.074	−2.773
3	−2.219	−3.77	−3.152	−2.846
2	−2.092	−3.77	−3.222	−2.912
1	−2.08	−3.77	−3.283	−2.968

Table 6A.5   (continued)

Lags	DF–GLS test statistic	1% critical value	5% critical value	10% critical value
ln(P/K)				
9	−1.147	−3.77	−2.712	−2.398
8	−1.339	−3.77	−2.768	−2.464
7	−1.269	−3.77	−2.836	−2.537
6	−1.549	−3.77	−2.912	−2.615
5	−1.859	−3.77	−2.993	−2.695
4	−1.823	−3.77	−3.074	−2.773
3	−1.893	−3.77	−3.152	−2.846
2	−2.115	−3.77	−3.222	−2.912
1	−2.266	−3.77	−3.283	−2.968
ln(π^F/K)				
9	−1.712	−3.77	−2.712	−2.398
8	−1.506	−3.77	−2.768	−2.464
7	−1.413	−3.77	−2.836	−2.537
6	−1.422	−3.77	−2.912	−2.615
5	−1.518	−3.77	−2.993	−2.695
4	−1.433	−3.77	−3.074	−2.773
3	−1.595	−3.77	−3.152	−2.846
2	−1.428	−3.77	−3.222	−2.912
1	−1.769	−3.77	−3.283	−2.968

Table 6A.6   Phillips–Perron unit root test

	Test statistic	1% critical value	5% critical value	10% critical value
ln(*I/K*)				
Z(rho)	−14.878	−18.424	−13.076	−10.56
Z(t)	−3.159	−3.628	−2.95	−2.608
ln(*π/K*)				
Z(rho)	−5.696	−18.424	−13.076	−10.56
Z(t)	−1.744	−3.628	−2.95	−2.608
ln(*GVA/K*)				
Z(rho)	−0.678	−18.424	−13.076	−10.56
Z(t)	−1.502	−3.628	−2.95	−2.608
ln(*D/K*)				
Z(rho)	−2.696	−18.424	−13.076	−10.56
Z(t)	−1.226	−3.628	−2.95	−2.608
ln(*P/K*)				
Z(rho)	−4.122	−18.424	−13.076	−10.56
Z(t)	−1.736	−3.628	−2.95	−2.608
ln(*π^F/K*)				
Z(rho)	−1.769	−18.424	−13.076	−10.56
Z(t)	−1.214	−3.628	−2.95	−2.608

Table 6A.7   Augmented Dickey–Fuller unit root test for differenced variables

		Test statistics	1% critical	5% critical	10% critical
ln(*I/K*)	Z(t)	−6.274	−3.628	−2.95	−2.608
ln(*π/K*)	Z(t)	−5.005	−3.628	−2.95	−2.608
ln(*GVA/K*)	Z(t)	−3.636	−3.628	−2.95	−2.608
ln(*D/K*)	Z(t)	−4.114	−3.628	−2.95	−2.608
ln(*P/K*)	Z(t)	−6.609	−3.628	−2.95	−2.608
ln(*π^F/K*)	Z(t)	−7.81	−3.628	−2.95	−2.608

Notes:
H_0: Variable contains a unit root.
H_1: Variable was generated by a stationary process.

Table 6A.8   DF–GLS unit root test for differenced variables

Lags	DF–GLS test statistic	1% critical value	5% critical value	10% critical value
ln(*I/K*)				
9	−2.536	−3.77	−2.712	−2.398
8	−2.985	−3.77	−2.768	−2.464
7	−2.071	−3.77	−2.836	−2.537
6	−1.919	−3.77	−2.912	−2.615
5	−2.788	−3.77	−2.993	−2.695
4	−2.288	−3.77	−3.074	−2.773
3	−3.537	−3.77	−3.152	−2.846
2	−4.099	−3.77	−3.222	−2.912
1	−5.133	−3.77	−3.283	−2.968
ln(*π/K*)				
9	−2.133	−3.77	−2.712	−2.398
8	−2.632	−3.77	−2.768	−2.464
7	−3.154	−3.77	−2.836	−2.537
6	−2.699	−3.77	−2.912	−2.615
5	−3.244	−3.77	−2.993	−2.695
4	−2.857	−3.77	−3.074	−2.773
3	−3.344	−3.77	−3.152	−2.846
2	−3.695	−3.77	−3.222	−2.912
1	−4.921	−3.77	−3.283	−2.968
ln(*GVA/K*)				
9	−1.181	−3.77	−2.712	−2.398
8	−1.605	−3.77	−2.768	−2.464
7	−1.646	−3.77	−2.836	−2.537
6	−1.869	−3.77	−2.912	−2.615
5	−2.063	−3.77	−2.993	−2.695
4	−1.335	−3.77	−3.074	−2.773
3	−1.402	−3.77	−3.152	−2.846
2	−1.493	−3.77	−3.222	−2.912
1	−1.984	−3.77	−3.283	−2.968
ln(*D/K*)				
9	−1.795	−3.77	−2.712	−2.398
8	−2.219	−3.77	−2.768	−2.464
7	−2.012	−3.77	−2.836	−2.537
6	−2.179	−3.77	−2.912	−2.615
5	−1.839	−3.77	−2.993	−2.695
4	−2.004	−3.77	−3.074	−2.773
3	−2.156	−3.77	−3.152	−2.846
2	−2.608	−3.77	−3.222	−2.912
1	−3.125	−3.77	−3.283	−2.968

Table 6A.8   (*continued*)

Lags	DF–GLS test statistic	1% critical value	5% critical value	10% critical value
ln(*P/K*)				
9	−1.438	−3.77	−2.712	−2.398
8	−2.303	−3.77	−2.768	−2.464
7	−2.275	−3.77	−2.836	−2.537
6	−2.95	−3.77	−2.912	−2.615
5	−2.883	−3.77	−2.993	−2.695
4	−2.807	−3.77	−3.074	−2.773
3	−3.337	−3.77	−3.152	−2.846
2	−3.964	−3.77	−3.222	−2.912
1	−4.517	−3.77	−3.283	−2.968
ln(π^F/K)				
9	−2.157	−3.77	−2.712	−2.398
8	−2.357	−3.77	−2.768	−2.464
7	−2.683	−3.77	−2.836	−2.537
6	−3.055	−3.77	−2.912	−2.615
5	−3.309	−3.77	−2.993	−2.695
4	−3.334	−3.77	−3.074	−2.773
3	−4.029	−3.77	−3.152	−2.846
2	−4.072	−3.77	−3.222	−2.912
1	−6.042	−3.77	−3.283	−2.968

Table 6A.9   Phillips–Perron unit root test for differenced variables

	Test statistic	1% critical value	5% critical value	10% critical value
ln(*I/K*)				
Z(rho)	−38.01	−18.424	−13.076	−10.56
Z(t)	−6.279	−3.628	−2.95	−2.608
ln(*π/K*)				
Z(rho)	−29.427	−18.424	−13.076	−10.56
Z(t)	−4.873	−3.628	−2.95	−2.608
ln(*GVA/K*)				
Z(rho)	−20.647	−18.424	−13.076	−10.56
Z(t)	−3.65	−3.628	−2.95	−2.608
ln(*D/K*)				
Z(rho)	−24.698	−18.424	−13.076	−10.56
Z(t)	−4.084	−3.628	−2.95	−2.608
ln(*P/K*)				
Z(rho)	−40.464	−18.424	−13.076	−10.56
Z(t)	−6.648	−3.628	−2.95	−2.608
ln(*π^F/K*)				
Z(rho)	−48.158	−18.424	−13.076	−10.56
Z(t)	−7.955	−3.628	−2.95	−2.608

APPENDIX 6B: TIME-SERIES PLOTS OF
REGRESSION VARIABLES

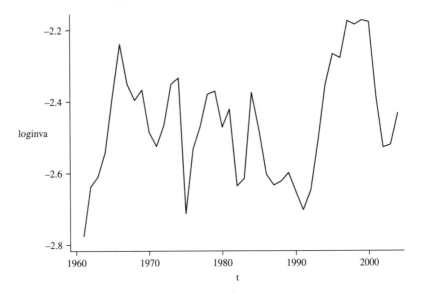

Figure 6B.1   ln(*I*/*K*)

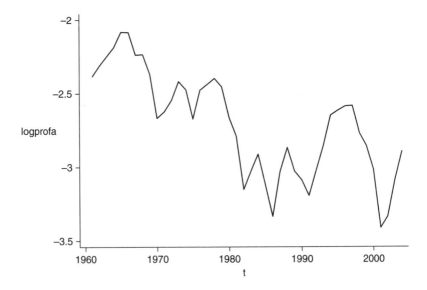

Figure 6B.2   ln(π/*K*)

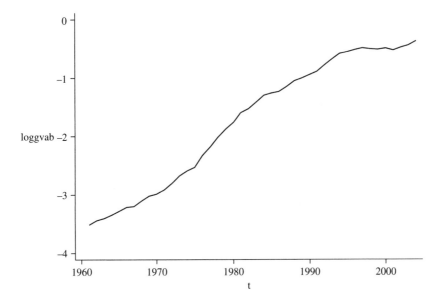

Figure 6B.3 ln(*GVA/K*)

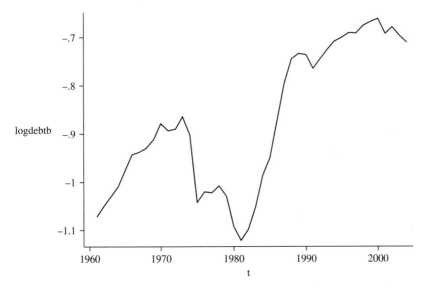

Figure 6B.4 ln(*D/K*)

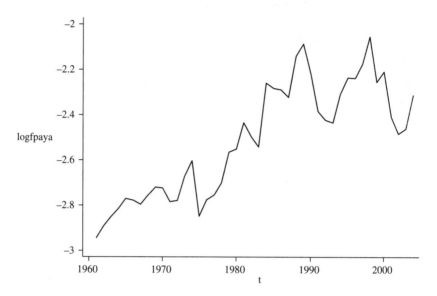

Figure 6B.5 ln(*P*/*K*)

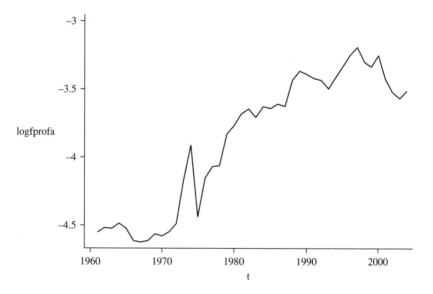

Figure 6B.6 ln(π^{F}/*K*)

7. Financialization and investment: firm-level analysis

Analysis of aggregate time-series data provides initial support for the view that financialization has negative effects on NFC investment in real capital. In this chapter, I carry on the analysis to firm level and empirically test the impact of financialization on a large sample of nonfinancial firms for the period 1973–2003. I use different sector, industry and size specifications to examine the robustness of the findings. While most results are robust across these different specifications, I identify different effects of financialization on firms from different sectors and sizes. For example, while the negative effect of financialization through increased financial payout ratios is unambiguous across industries, and in small and large firms, the negative effect of increased financial profits is most obvious in large corporations which were arguably more involved in financial investments than small corporations. The contribution of this chapter is unique in that it makes use of a firm-level database to test these hypotheses for the first time. Earlier analyses, both Stockhammer (2004) and the previous chapter are limited to aggregate data analyses, which may have prevented the identification of cross-firm differences. Firm-level data permit the analysis of the effects and extent of financialization on firms of different sizes and in different sectors and/or industries. Just as important, firm-level data make it possible to analyse the characteristics of large firms, which are most likely to be affected by financialization.

STATISTICAL SPECIFICATION

The model discussed in Chapter 5 is appropriate for the analysis of the effects of financialization at the firm level as it considers the pursuit of financial security as a significant constraint on managerial decision-making and the financialization literature suggests that there have been significant changes in terms of the financial security of the firm. Moreover, it accounts for the effects of increasing financial investments of the firms through the use of a proxy for financial profits made by the firm. The equation estimated in this chapter takes the following form:

$$\ln(I_{it}/K_{i,t-1}) = \alpha_0 + \alpha_1 \ln(\pi/K)_{i,t-1} + \alpha_2 \ln(S/K)_{i,t-1} + \alpha_3 \ln(D/K)_{i,t-1}$$

$$+ \alpha_4 \ln(P/K)_{i,t-1} + \alpha_5 \ln(\pi^F/K)_{i,t-1} \tag{7.1}$$

where ln is a logarithmic function, $\alpha_0 \ldots \alpha_5$ are parameters, the i subscript denotes the firm, and the t subscript denotes the time period. I is investment in fixed assets, K is capital stock, π is operating profits, S is the sales, D is total debt, π^F is the financial income, and P is the sum of interest payments, dividend payments and stock buybacks.

As in Chapter 6, the regression variables are scaled by beginning of period capital stock to correct for heteroscedasticity, which is a common practice in investment studies that use firm-level data.[1] Logarithmic forms are used to account for potential non-linearities in the relationships among the explanatory variables and the rate of investment. In order to control for the dynamic effects, I include the first lag of the investment-to-capital ratio in the regressions below.[2]

The model tests for two effects of financialization – through the π^F and P variables – on the investment behavior of NFCs while controlling for other determinants of investment. First, increased financial investment and increased financial profit opportunities may have crowded out real investment by changing the incentives of firm managers and directing funds away from real investment. Second, increased payments to the financial markets may have impeded real investment by decreasing available internal funds, shortening the planning horizons of the firm management and increasing uncertainty. Before going into a discussion of the empirical results, I discuss the properties of the data set and explain the sample selection criteria in the next section.

DATA

The data that I use come from Standard and Poor's 'Compustat Annual Industrial Database.' This provides panel data for a large number of firms. The period covered is from 1972 to 2003, 1972 being the first year when the full set of data items used for this study is reported. This period is appropriate for the purposes of this study. As pointed out earlier, there has been an increase in financial incomes, payments and assets in the post-1980 era, while at the same time the rate of capital accumulation has declined compared with the earlier post-war period. I include all nonfinancial firms from the database (the Standard Industry Classification (SIC) codes 6000-6799 are excluded as they refer to financial firms). However, in order to provide comparability with other investment studies, which in most cases take the manufacturing sector as their sample, I pay specific attention to the manufacturing sector (SIC codes 2000-3999). The results for the manufacturing sector are important since it represents a significant part of the production side of the macroeconomy and is important in affecting business cycles. I compare the results with the entire set of non-manufacturing firms.

Financialization is a complicated process that may affect different corporations in different ways. Macroeconomic data, although useful in identifying general trends, fail to pick up the heterogeneity in firm behavior. Firm-level analysis provides an opportunity to control for firm-specific effects. The use of data on individual firms has many advantages compared with using aggregate time-series data. Biases due to aggregation can be avoided. In addition, the cross-sectional variation in panel data increases the precision of parameter estimates while taking the heterogeneity across firms into account. Moreover, 'the availability of micro data allows models to move beyond the notion of a representative firm, so that cross-firm differences in the investment decision process itself can be investigated' (Blundell et al. 1996: 685). The possibility of differentiating between large and small firms, which have potentially different behaviors, is another advantage of panel data.

The sample I use here is an unbalanced panel, as a firm is not required to have observations for all the years in the period. Using a balanced panel sample could introduce certain biases in the sense that only firms that have survived for the whole period would be in the sample and I would have to delete a significant number of firms just because data were not reported on certain items for some years. Furthermore, the coverage of the Compustat database increases over time. One can take advantage of the availability of more firms in recent years by utilizing an unbalanced panel. I require a firm to have at least ten years of observations after cleaning the missing observations for the regression variables to be included in the sample. In addition, I exclude firms that have had permanently negative profit rates for the years that they are in the sample.

A common problem with firm data is the existence of large outliers, especially when the variables are expressed in the form of ratios (Chirinko et al. 1999). A significant degree of heterogeneity among the firms might generate large outliers which can bias the empirical results. To eliminate this problem, I apply a two-step procedure and exclude the outliers. In the first step, I calculate firm means for each regression variable. Second, I exclude the firms whose means fall in the 1 percent or the 99 percent tails of the distribution of the variable in the sample. Following Chirinko et al. (1999), I do not delete outliers for the dependent variable to avoid a censored regression bias.[3]

Variables used are directly taken from the Compustat database. I is 'capital expenditures' (Compustat data item 128); K is 'net property, plant and equipment' (Compustat data item 8); π is 'operating income' (Compustat data item 8); S is 'sales' (Compustat data item12); P is the sum of 'interest expense,' 'cash dividend' and 'purchase of [firm's own] common and preferred stock' (Compustat data items 15, 127 and 115); D is 'long-term debt-total' (Compustat data item 9); and π^F is the sum of 'interest income' and 'equity in net earnings' (Compustat data items 62 and 55).[4] The size variable used is 'total assets' (Compustat data item 6).

The nominal values of all the variables are deflated in order to obtain real values. I use the price index of investment goods to deflate capital expenditures and the capital stock. Other variables are deflated by the GNP deflator. As noted above, the regression variables are scaled by the capital stock at the beginning of the period in order to correct for heteroscedasticity. Table 7.1 presents summary statistics for the regression variables. It shows that there are large variations within and across firms.

REGRESSION RESULTS

The dynamic investment model in Equation (2) is estimated using the Arellano–Bond 'generalized method of moments' (GMM) estimation technique. GMM eliminates the potential endogeneity problems caused by the inclusion of a lagged value of the independent variable among explanatory variables. To eliminate unobservable firm-fixed effects such as technology and managerial ability that would have an effect on the investment behavior of the firm (Ndikumana 1999: 465), explanatory variables are first-differenced and year dummies are used to account for unobservable time-specific factors.

Results of the regression analyses are presented in Tables 7.2 and 7.3. Table 7.2 presents results by sector and industry: all nonfinancial firms, manufacturing firms and non-manufacturing firms. Manufacturing firms are further divided into durable and non-durable goods producing industries.[5] This split would potentially account for the effects of business cycles since durables industries are considered to be more sensitive to the business cycles. Within these sectors and industries, results for subsamples of large and small firms are also reported. Table 7.3 takes disaggregation by size a step further and presents results for five different firm sizes within the manufacturing firms.

Real variables
I start by examining whether the base variables in the investment model are appropriate for explaining investment. In general, the real-side

Table 7.1 Summary statistics

Variable	Manufacturing firms			All nonfinancial firms			Non-manufacturing firms		
	Mean	Std. Dev.	Obs.	Mean	Std. Dev.	Obs.	Mean	Std. Dev.	Obs.
Investment									
overall	0.281	0.390	N=19054	0.263	0.370	N=36356	0.244	0.348	N=17371
between		0.159	n=815		0.164	n=1573		0.167	n=759
within		0.364	T-bar=23.3		0.339	T-bar=23.1		0.311	T-bar=22.8
Profit									
overall	0.424	0.847	N=19051	0.350	0.780	N=36351	0.269	0.997	N=17369
between		0.464	n=815		0.447	n=1573		0.404	n=759
within		0.742	T-bar=23.3		0.669	T-bar=23.1		0.923	T-bar=22.8
Sales									
overall	7.148	6.989	N=19054	6.925	9.767	N=36356	6.882	12.985	N=17371
between		5.534	n=815		8.307	n=1573		11.246	n=759
within		4.575	T-bar=23.3		5.809	T-bar=23.1		7.293	T-bar=22.8
Long-term debt									
overall	0.793	1.407	N=18214	0.819	1.609	N=34758	0.849	1.774	N=16612
between		0.857	n=815		1.056	n=1573		1.212	n=759
within		1.200	T-bar=22.3		1.322	T-bar=22.0		1.418	T-bar=21.8
Financial payouts									
overall	0.264	0.406	N=18659	0.238	0.454	N=35712	0.211	0.498	N=17122
between		0.214	n=815		0.250	n=1573		0.276	n=759
within		0.354	T-bar=22.8		0.392	T-bar=22.7		0.430	T-bar=22.5
Financial profits									
overall	0.097	0.234	N=16944	0.083	0.226	N=32068	0.070	0.251	N=15184
between		0.131	n=815		0.121	n=1573		0.122	n=759
within		0.195	T-bar=20.7		0.191	T-bar=20.3		0.220	T-bar=20

Note: All variables are deflated by the capital stock.

Table 7.2   Estimation results by industry and sector

Dependent variable: $(I/K)_t$	Nonfinancial			Manufacturing		
	All	Large[a]	Small[b]	All	Large[a]	Small[b]
$(I/K)_{t-1}$	.134***	.263***	.095***	.103***	.235***	.058
	(.017)	(.052)	(.022)	(.021)	(.060)	(.031)
$(S/K)_{t-1}$	.142***	.064***	.155***	.159***	.059***	.175***
	(.009)	(.008)	(.014)	(.014)	(.009)	(.022)
$(\pi/K)_{t-1}$	.038***	.076***	.049***	.046***	.099***	.058**
	(.010)	(.017)	(.012)	(.013)	(.023)	(.020)
$(P/K)_{t-1}$	−.036*	−.061***	−.042**	−.023	−.070**	−.055*
	(.016)	(.018)	(.015)	(.016)	(.024)	(.022)
$(\pi^F/K)_{t-1}$	.055	−.084***	.061	.022	−.098*	.028
	(.050)	(.025)	(.071)	(.058)	(.040)	(.084)
$(D/K)_{t-1}$	−.033***	−.013**	−.056**	−.027*	−.012	−.054***
	(.009)	(.005)	(.020)	(.012)	(.011)	(.011)
Observations	24719	2476	6018	13076	1371	3147
Firms	1572	258	594	815	126	319
Pr>Jn	.01	1.00	.45	.01	1.00	1.00
Pr>|m1|	.00	.00	.00	.00	.00	.00
Pr>|m2|	.21	.13	.12	.17	.16	.13

Notes:
Estimates are obtained by the Arellano–Bond one-step difference GMM. The instrument set includes all available instruments, beginning from $t-2$. The coefficients for the year fixed effects and for the constant term are not reported. Robust standard errors are in parentheses. P-values for the Hansen–Sargan test of overidentifying restrictions (Jn) and Arellano–Bond tests of first order (m1) and second order (m2) autocorrelation in the errors are obtained from two-step estimations. * indicates significance at 10 percent, ** significance at 5 percent and *** significance at 1 percent.
(a) A firm is considered large if the size of its total assets is in the upper 10 percent distribution of the total assets for the sample.
(b) A firm is considered small if the size of its total assets is in the lower 25 percent distribution of the total assets for the sample.

variables, lagged rate of investment, rate of profit and sales, have the expected signs and for almost all specifications have statistical significance. The general specification of the investment function seem appropriate to capture the real-side variables' effects on investment and hence provide a good base on which the effects of financialization can be tested. The coefficients of the profit and sales variables, which are proxies for real constraints, have the expected positive signs for all specifications. They are also statistically significant with a few exceptions. The size of the coefficient on the sales variable is larger for small firms, both for

Durables		Non-durables		Non-manufacturing		
Large [a]	Small [b]	Large [a]	Small [b]	All	Large [a]	Small [b]
.243***	.068**	.345***	.093*	.177***	.236***	.104***
(.070)	(.024)	(.051)	(.038)	(.027)	(.044)	(.030)
.070***	.170***	.041***	.109***	.091***	.031**	.082***
(.012)	(.020)	(.007)	(.014)	(.008)	(.011)	(.010)
.086**	.046**	.056**	.019	.011	.079***	.026
(.030)	(.018)	(.017)	(.033)	(.018)	(.023)	(.020)
−.092*	−.037*	−.015	−.028	−.061	−.066***	−.084
(.043)	(.017)	(.015)	(.018)	(.032)	(.019)	(.064)
−.050	.002	−.036	.202*	.013	−.010	−.112
(.044)	(.081)	(.057)	(.088)	(.097)	(.027)	(.139)
−.018	−.037*	.001	−.043***	−.031**	−.017	−.031
(.015)	(.019)	(.007)	(.009)	(.011)	(.009)	(.023)
820	4576	551	1978	11 718	1143	2836
75	371	51	163	758	131	298
1.00	1.00	1.00	1.00	.00	1.00	1.00
.00	.00	.74	.00	.00	.00	.00
.01	.17	.02	.64	.12	.90	.22

manufacturing and non-manufacturing firms. For the whole sample, we observe a larger size for the coefficient of the profit variable in larger firms.

In all regressions except for small manufacturing firms we observe a significant dynamic component represented by the first lag of the investment to capital ratio. The positive effect is larger and statistically more significant for large firms. This is consistent with the argument that for large firms, investment projects tend to run over a longer period and hence high investment in the previous year would be associated with high investment in the current year. Overall, the first lag of investment to capital ratio is positive and significant for all NFCs as shown in Table 7.2. This effect is statistically significant for the manufacturing sector as a whole and within it, for both durable and non-durable goods producing industries. The effect remains positive for non-manufacturing firms and we also observe significant positive effects of lagged investment in smaller firms in the non-manufacturing sector. Table 7.3 shows the significant effects for large manufacturing firms.

Table 7.3   Estimation results by size for manufacturing sector

Dependent variable: $(I/K)_t$	(1)	(2)	(3)	(4)	(5)
$(I/K)_{t-1}$	.264***	.235***	.233***	.058	.079***
	(.065)	(.060)	(.038)	(.031)	(.023)
$(S/K)_{t-1}$	.051***	.059***	.081***	.175***	.164***
	(.008)	(.009)	(.009)	(.022)	(.017)
$(\pi/K)_{t-1}$	.107***	.099***	.018	.058**	.050**
	(.032)	(.023)	(.020)	(.020)	(.016)
$(P/K)_{t-1}$	−.090***	−.070**	−.015	−.055	−.032
	(.026)	(.024)	(.011)	(.034)	(.023)
$(\pi^F/K)_{t-1}$	−.086***	−.098*	−.022	.028	.040
	(.028)	(.040)	(.031)	(.084)	(.072)
$(D/K)_{t-1}$	.002	−.012	−.005	−.054***	−.039*
	(.012)	(.011)	(.008)	(.011)	(.017)
Observations	693	1371	3213	3147	6554
Firms	72	126	271	319	534
Pr>Jn	1.00	1.00	1.00	1.00	.31
Pr>|m1|	.00	.00	.00	.00	.00
Pr>|m2|	.42	.16	.80	.13	.18

Notes: Estimates are obtained by the Arellano–Bond one-step difference GMM. The instrument set includes all available instruments, beginning from $t-2$. The coefficients for the year fixed effects and for the constant term are not reported. Robust standard errors are in parentheses. Estimates are obtained by the Arellano–Bond one-step difference GMM. The instrument set includes all available instruments, beginning from $t-2$. The coefficients for the year fixed effects and for the constant term are not reported. Robust standard errors are in parentheses. P-values for the Hansen–Sargan test of overidentifying restrictions (Jn) and Arellano–Bond tests of first order (m1) and second order (m2) autocorrelation in the errors are obtained from two-step estimations. * indicates significance at 10 percent, ** significance at 5 percent and *** significance at 1 percent.
(1) Total assets in the upper 5 percent of the distribution.
(2) Total assets in the upper 10 percent of the distribution.
(3) Total assets in the upper 25 percent of the distribution.
(4) Total assets in the lower 25 percent of the distribution.
(5) Total assets in the lower 50 percent of the distribution.

Long-term debt

On the financial side, the long-term debt-to-capital ratio, which is a proxy for the long-term financial robustness of the firm, has a negative and statistically significant coefficient when all NFCs are considered. This indicates that higher levels of debt constrain investment as they increase the financial fragility of the firms. In terms of its statistical significance this term does not perform as well as the real variables discussed. An interesting note perhaps is that, as shown in Table 7.3, the long-term debt variable has a positive but small impact on the investment behavior of the larger manufacturing firms and is statistically insignificant. In general, high long-term debt-to-capital ratios do constrain the investment behavior of the firm. The statistical results show that as the long-term indebtedness of the firm increases it may have a negative effect on investment.

Financial payouts

Turning back to the focus of this chapter, I next examine the results for the two financialization variables employed, the financial profit and financial payout ratios. The financial payout variable has the negative coefficient predicted by financialization theory and it is statistically significant in most subsamples, as Tables 7.2 and 7.3 show. When the sample is divided into small and large firms, the sign of the coefficient remains unchanged. Further, Table 7.2 shows that it is robust to different industry specifications under the manufacturing sector. In terms of the magnitude of the effect, we observe that it approaches those of sales and profit variables.

On the whole, these results support the hypothesis that increased financial payout ratios can impede real investment by allocating funds away from real investment and by shortening the planning horizons of the NFCs. This finding is in contrast with the neoclassical investment theory, in which it is the expected profitability of investment that drives investment decisions and every investment project that is profitable would find funding. There is no room in neoclassical theory for an argument that higher financial payments reduce capital accumulation due to a shortage of funds. However, statistical findings presented here support the argument that increased financial payout ratios decrease investment by either directing funds away from investment or by shortening the managerial planning horizon as firms are either trying to meet the short-term return expectations of the financial markets or as the managers are trying to increase the short-term value of the firm and hence maximize their returns from stock options.

Financial profits

The financial profits variable employed in the regressions provides interesting results that are sensitive to firm size. We observe negative and significant coefficients for this variable for large firms across different sectors. This provides strong empirical support for the financialization hypothesis, which reflects an insight not available from either neoclassical or new-Keynesian theories.

Nevertheless, the effect for small firms is positive. This is not entirely surprising. A positive coefficient on the financial profits variable would be consistent with liquidity-based investment theories or with the financing constraint hypothesis. Income from financial investments can be used to finance real investment in the future. However, we observe this only for small firms. Given that small firms are not involved in financial investments as much as large firms, their financial holdings (and hence the interest income – the main financial income they have – derived from these) can be correlated positively with investment if small firms are saving up before undertaking large investments, a result predicted by the new-Keynesian theories of investment. However, the robust and significant results for large firms suggest that increased financial investments by these firms do have a negative effect on real investment. For large firms the coefficient of the financial profits variable is negative and statistically significant, indicating that for these firms, past financial investment does not support current real investment. This is consistent with the argument that increased financial profits reflect a change in the managerial preferences towards short-termism and financial investment and hence affect real investment adversely.

In short, strong evidence has been found that financialization has negative effects on firm investment behavior, especially for large firms. The financial payout variable has negative and statistically significant coefficients for almost all specifications and the financial income variable has negative and significant coefficients for the larger firms. These results provide the first firm-level evidence regarding the potential negative effects of financialization on investment.

SUMMARY OF THE ANALYSIS

This chapter analysed the potential effects of financialization on the investment behavior of NFCs. Financialization has two aspects. On the one hand, NFCs increase their financial investments relative to their real investments and hence derive an increasing part of their income from financial sources. On the other hand, NFCs are under increased pressure from the financial markets to increase the amount of funds they return to these markets. Hence, NFCs transfer an increasing part of their earnings to financial markets in the forms of dividends and stock buybacks, in addition to interest payments.

These two aspects of financialization could have negative effects on real capital accumulation. First, increased financial investments can crowd out real investment by directing funds away from it into financial investment and increased financial profits can change the incentives of the firm management regarding investment decisions. Therefore, the first hypothesis developed was that high financial profit opportunities lead to higher financial investment and result in a decline in real investment. Second, increased financial payments can decrease the funds available for real capital accumulation while the need to increase financial payments can decrease the amount of available funds, shorten the managerial planning horizon and increase uncertainty. Hence, the second hypothesis developed was that the demand for increased financial payout ratios leaves firms with fewer funds to invest, as well as a shortening of the planning horizon of its management and increasing uncertainty, which leads to lower levels of investment.

A model of NFC investment including variables to account for these two impacts was tested by using firm-level data. The findings indicate a negative relationship between financialization and capital accumulation, especially for large firms. The results support the view that financialization has negative implications for firm investment behavior. Although the results are not necessarily conclusive, they represent a new attempt to examine the relationship between financialization and investment at the firm level.

The negative effects of financialization on investment confirm the concern that financialization could be slowing down the accumulation of capital. Although the findings do not lend themselves to easy policy conclusions, they indicate that overall, the nature of the relationship between financial markets and NFCs does not necessarily support productive investment. On the contrary, it might be creating impediments. I discuss the relevance of these results for the financialization era in general in the next chapter.

NOTES

1. See Kuh (1963), Eisner (1960), Fazzari et al. (1988) and Carpenter et al. (1995) for earlier uses of the method.
2. See Kopcke and Brauman (2001) on the significance of this term in explaining investment. The lagged values of investment account for dynamic effects such as gestation time for investment (investment projects taking more time than one period) and inertia (higher (lower) investment leading to higher (lower) investment).
3. See Greene (2003: 761–3) for a discussion of censored data and their distribution. Deleting outliers for the dependent variable does not change the results obtained in any significant way.

4. Unfortunately, it is not possible to obtain a variable that reflects all financial incomes of the firm. For this reason, I use the sum of interest income and equity in net earnings which is the income from holdings of unconsolidated subsidiaries. Compustat does not report firm's income from capital gains and dividends received.
5. Durables are composed of industries with SIC codes 20-23 and 26-31. Non-durables are composed of industries with SIC codes 24, 25 and 32-38. The category labeled in Compustat as 'miscellaneous' contains heterogeneous industries and is not included in these regressions.

8. Conclusion

Recent decades have witnessed an explosion in everything financial. Financial markets have grown enormously in both size and significance. They have started to command ever greater resources and have acquired an important role in the governance of NFCs. The share of income allocated to financial institutions has skyrocketed, while nonfinancial institutions have also increasingly become involved in investments in financial assets and financial subsidiaries. All these developments have been discussed extensively in the ever-growing financialization literature. In the first chapter of this book, I drew attention to the vague and imprecise nature of the concept and after a review of different definitions and usages of it; I offered a clear definition of financialization, suitable for analytical use. Here, financialization was defined at two levels: At the general level, financialization refers to an increase in the size and significance of financial markets, transactions and institutions. At a narrower level, I used financialization to designate changes in the relationship between the nonfinancial corporate sector and financial markets. These latter changes include, first, an increase in financial investments and hence financial incomes, of the NFCs; and second, an increase in financial market pressure on the management of NFCs and an associated rise in transfers made to financial markets in the forms of interest payments, dividend payments and stock buybacks.

In the second chapter, I documented various aspects of the rise of finance in the US economy through simple descriptive time-series statistics. The third chapter focused on contextualizing these changes within a historical framework. In the fourth chapter, I critically evaluated different perspectives on financialization in an attempt to uncover the limits of our understanding of the phenomenon. This chapter brought forward some important questions that I will reiterate here shortly. In sum, the first four chapters of this work are centered on the question of how to understand the process of financialization as part of a historical and complicated process. I outlined an initial framework for understanding the causes and consequences of financialization of the economy.

The rest of the book discussed the impact of financialization on the capital accumulation process in the nonfinancial corporate sector. After establishing the theoretical framework for analysing the relationship between financialization and capital accumulation in the fifth chapter, the sixth chapter provided aggregate time-series analysis of the US data and found that increased involvement of NFCs in financial investments and the increased pressure on these corporations to allocate ever higher shares of their earnings to the financial markets in the forms of interest payments, dividends and stock buybacks had a negative effect on the level of their real investments. However, aggregate analysis failed to provide conclusive results, while not being suitable for picking up the potentially diverse effects of financialization on different sets of firms. Therefore, in Chapter 7, I turned to a firm-level analysis. I found that the negative impact of increased financial incomes on real investment is confirmed for large firms and the results are robust to different samples of firms such as manufacturing and non-manufacturing firms. The negative impact of increased financial payout ratios is felt more by smaller firms across all sectors. Overall, these chapters provide theoretical and econometric evidence that financialization has negative effects on real capital accumulation.

The discussions in this book perhaps brought up more questions than they answer. I think these questions deserve further research and debate, if we want to improve our understanding of the dynamics of the current economic system and the financialization phenomenon that seems to dominate the system. I will recount the most important ones here again. The first question pertains to the issue of measuring financialization. Although we know that NFCs in the US and in some other parts of the world have increased their financial investments vastly in the last two decades, it is not 100 percent clear what types of financial investments these corporations undertake. An increasing portion of the financial asset holdings of the NFCs is classified as 'miscellaneous' in the statistical accounts. This problem is ignored in most accounts of financialization. Without knowing exactly what kind of financial investments these corporations undertake, analyses of the impacts of financialization on NFCs will remain incomplete. A better understanding of the nature of NFC financial investments would enhance our understanding of the implications of financialization for these firms. However, this task seems very difficult as major databases do not include this information and the firms bury most of these financial investment categories in the footnotes of hundreds of pages of annual reports.

An interesting question generated through the historical review of the evolution of financial markets is that of the similarities and contrasts between the finance capital era of the late 19th to early 20th centuries and the current era of financialization. Historical accounts of the finance capital era point to the 'positive' role played by bankers and financiers in coordinating economic activity in the late 19th century and early in the 20th century. Financiers supported capital accumulation by forcing NFCs to avoid destructive competition and to take advantage of the potential benefits of the economies of scale that their industries entailed. Here positive is defined in terms of financiers' contribution to the capital accumulation; of course they did this for their own interest, reflected by very high profit margins. However, what we observe in the financialization era is an increased pressure by financial markets and institutions on NFCs to increase payments made to financiers in the short-run and to distribute earnings to financial markets while downsizing the corporations. Combined with other problems that neoliberal policies bring about, such as a slow-down in aggregate demand and an increase in destructive competition, financialization of the current era seems to have had negative effects on capital accumulation. Findings presented in this book are certainly in line with most of the literature that emphasize negative effects of financialization on capital accumulation and growth. A thorough analysis of the parallels as well as contrasts between the previous financial expansion and the current one would certainly contribute to our understanding of the capitalist system, and in Arrighi's terms, its long cycles. It would also enhance our understanding of the role of finance within the global neoliberal order.

The discussion of different perspectives on financialization also uncovered important questions. First of all, the transition from a system with regulated financial markets into a system of unfettered finance is not well theorized in the literature. There are different points of view in this regard, some arguing that this transition is the result of structural changes in the economy while other authors emphasize the role of class dynamics and politics in this transition. A common theme in the literature is the role of the accumulation crisis of the 1970s. Many in the literature argue that financialization, together with liberalization and deregulation, was a response to this crisis. However, there are not many studies that theoretically or empirically discuss the relationship between capital accumulation and financialization. While this book provides a contribution toward this end, further research on this issue would certainly shed more light on the dynamics of the financialized era.

While this book presents evidence that financialization has negative effects on capital accumulation, increased involvement of NFCs in financial investments and the rising share of financial incomes in their total incomes could have the effect of increasing the potential fragility of these corporations, a point frequently visited by the business press, but rather neglected in the economics literature. At a broader level, the rapid increase in the sizes of financial markets and institutions also increases the fragility of the global economy. In a recent *Global Financial Stability Report*, the IMF (2006) expresses concern over the growth of hedge funds and credit derivatives and warns against 'financial turbulence' (pp. 74–5). The increased instability has been reflected by numerous financial crises since the 1990s. While these crises have been devastating for the economies affected by them, in most cases international finance capitalists gained from them and extended their reach by using these crises as an opportunity to further neoliberal restructuring in these countries.[1]

Implications of financialization on the labor relations within NFCs constitute another understudied topic. When financial markets started to push for higher payments by NFCs, this demand was increasingly met by corporate downsizing, cuts in the labor force and repressed wages. In addition, this era has also witnessed deterioration in the income distribution. Incomes of labor have been stagnant, while top managers and financiers have seen their incomes growing steadily. The role of financial markets in exacerbating income inequalities in the economy is a topic that deserves more attention. A very good starting point is provided by Duménil and Lévy (2004c) who show that under the financialized neoliberal order 'class relations remain as strong as ever . . . but that they have undergone a distinct reconfiguration. The cohesion between the uppermost layers . . . and a broader, subordinate tier of the "upper salaried classes" has been strengthened, and the gap between this bloc and the mass of the population below it has been widened' (p. 106).

A significant aspect of the financialization era has been the evolution in corporate governance practices toward elevating the interests of shareholders above those of other corporate stakeholders. These changes have also been promoted in the 'developing' countries. Studies of financialization and corporate governance changes, therefore, have critical implications for the 'developing' countries and more research on this issue would certainly contribute to the debates on development policies. Moreover, the empirical results of this book could have significant implications for 'developing' countries. Changes in financial market and corporate governance structures toward the US-style system are on the agenda in many countries.[2] However, a shift towards US-style financial markets and corporate governance would not necessarily increase prospects for economic growth. In this context, even mainstream corporate governance literature has recently found that the dominance of financial markets on NFCs can be associated with increased likelihood of firms restating earnings or committing fraud (Gillan 2006: 387). This in itself is not surprising but it should also be noted that the financialized capitalism does not involve a macro policy or strategy and hence 'booms lose their way if they are channeled into short-term speculation and arbitrage, rather than long-range investment' (Blackburn 2006: 68).[3] In short, to better understand the impact of financial markets on capital accumulation in both advanced and 'developing' countries, more studies of these relationships should be undertaken.

Moreover, for a long time, economists have been debating the merits of different financial systems. For example, Dore (2000) pointed out that financialization is an institutional configuration most strongly established in Anglo-American capitalism in which stock markets are more predominant. However, the effects of an increase in the size and power of the financial sector has not been discussed in this literature. The findings of the empirical chapters here have relevance for these debates, as I identify two potential channels through which financialization could impede investment in the US economy.

It is certainly possible to extend this list of questions and given the continuing dominance of finance in all sorts of economic activities, we can be sure that these questions and many more will continue to be analysed. It is hoped that this book may constitute a small contribution to the debates on the role of finance and help to improve our knowledge of the current state of the capitalist system.

NOTES

1. See Dufour and Orhangazi (2007a and 2007b) for detailed analyses on the consequences of financial crises. These works show that during most of the financial crises in the 'developing countries,' international finance capital benefits from the crisis by increasing its total assets in the country and income flows from it and structural changes imposed on the economy, in order to 'remedy' the situation, further the interests of capital in general.
2. See Soederberg (2003), Singh (2003) and Glen et al. (2000) for discussions of the promotion of US-style corporate governance in 'developing' countries.
3. More recently, in a similar vein, Kaplan et al. (2006) concluded that for Turkey, financial investments of real-sector firms may be crowding out real investment in the sector.

Bibliography

Aglietta, M. (2000), 'Shareholder value and corporate governance: some tricky questions,' *Economy and Society*, **29** (1), 146–59.

Aglietta, M. and R. Breton (2001), 'Financial systems, corporate control and capital accumulation,' *Economy and Society*, **30** (4), 433–66.

Akyüz, Y. and K. Boratav (2005), 'The Making of the Turkish Crisis,' in G. Epstein (ed.), *Financialization and the World Economy*, Cheltenham, UK and Northampton, MA, USA: Edward Elgar.

Allen, F. and D. Gale (1994), *Financial Innovation and Risk Sharing*, Cambridge, MA: MIT Press.

Allen, F. and D. Gale (2000), *Comparing Financial Systems*, Cambridge, MA: MIT Press.

Allen, F. and R. Michaely (1995), 'Dividend policy,' in R.A. Jarrow, V. Maksimovic and W.T. Ziemba (eds), *Finance, Handbooks in Operations Research and Management Science*, vol. 9, Amsterdam: Elsevier, pp. 793–839.

Amin, S. (1996), 'The challenge of globalization,' *Review of International Political Economy*, **3** (2), 216–59.

Amin, S. (2003), *Obsolescent Capitalism*, London and New York: Zed Books.

Amin, S. (2004), *The Liberal Virus: Permanent War and the Americanization of the World*, New York: Monthly Review Press.

Arrighi, G. (1994), *The Long Twentieth Century: Money, Power, and the Origins of Our Times*, London: Verso.

Arrighi, G. (2003), 'The social and political economy of global turbulence,' *New Left Review*, **20** (March–April), 5–71.

Arrighi, G. (2005), 'Hegemony unraveling-2,' *New Left Review*, (May–June), 83–116.

Arrighi, G. and B. Silver (1999), *Chaos and Governance in the Modern World System*, Minneapolis, MN: University of Minnesota Press.

Arrighi, G., P. Hui, K. Ray and T.E. Reifer (1999), 'Geopolitics and high finance,' in G. Arrighi and B. Silver (eds), *Chaos and Governance in the Modern World System*, Minneapolis, MN: University of Minnesota Press, pp. 15–96.

Arrighi, G., T. Hamashita and M. Selden (2003), *The Resurgence of East Asia: 500, 150 and 50 year Perspectives*, New York: Routledge.

136   *Bibliography*

Babb, S. (2005), 'The rise of the new money doctors in Mexico,' in G. Epstein (ed.), *Financialization and the World Economy*, Cheltenham, UK and Northampton, MA, USA: Edward Elgar, pp. 243–59.

Baker, G. and G. Smith (1998), *The New Financial Capitalists: Kohlberg Kravis Roberts and the Creation of Corporate Value*, New York: Cambridge University Press.

Baker, H.K., G.E. Powell and E.T. Veit (2002a), 'Revisiting the dividend puzzle,' *Review of Financial Economics*, **11**, 241–61.

Baker, H.K., G.E. Powell and E.T. Veit (2002b), 'Why companies use open-market repurchases: a managerial perspective,' *Quarterly Review of Economics and Finance*, **43** (3), 483–504.

Baskin, J.B. and P.J. Miranti, Jr. (1997), *A History of Corporate Finance*, Cambridge: Cambridge University Press.

Berle, A. and G. Means (1932), *The Modern Corporation and Private Property*, New York: Commerce Clearing House.

Bhagat S. and R.H. Jefferis (2002), *The Econometrics of Corporate Governance Studies*, Cambridge, MA: MIT Press.

Bhaskar, V. and A. Glyn (1995), 'Investment and profitability: the evidence from the advanced countries,' in G. Epstein and H. Gintis (eds), *Macroeconomics After the Conservative Era: Studies in Investment, Saving and Finance*, Cambridge: Cambridge University Press.

Binswanger, M. (1999), *Stock Markets, Speculative Bubbles and Economic Growth*, Cheltenham, UK and Northampton, MA, USA: Edward Elgar.

Bivens, J. and C. Weller (2004), 'Institutional shareholder concentration, corporate governance changes and diverging fortunes of capital and labor,' paper presented at the Center for Economic Policy Analysis conference on 'Pension Fund Capitalism and the Crisis of Old-Age Security in the United States' held at the New School University, 10-11 September, New York.

Blackburn, R. (2006), 'Finance and the fourth dimension,' *New Left Review*, **39**, 39–70.

Blecker, R. (2005), 'Financial globalization, exchange rates, and international trade,' in G. Epstein (ed.), *Financialization and the World Economy*, Cheltenham, UK and Northampton, MA, USA: Edward Elgar, pp. 183–219.

Blundell, R., S. Bond and C. Meghir (1996), 'Econometric models of company investment,' in L. Matyas and P. Sevestre (eds), *The Econometrics of Panel Data*, Dordrecht, Netherlands: Kluwer Academic Publishers, pp. 388–413.

Bottomore, T. (1983), *A Dictionary of Marxist Thought*, Cambridge, MA: Harvard University Press.

Boyer, R. (2000), 'Is a finance-led growth regime a viable alternative to Fordism? A preliminary analysis,' *Economy and Society*, **29** (1), 111–45.

Boyer, R. (2004), *The Future of Economic Growth: As New Becomes Old*, Cheltenham, UK and Northampton, MA, USA: Edward Elgar.

Braudel, F. (1984), *Civilization and Capitalism*, New York: Harper & Row.

Bruck, C. (1988), *The Predators' Ball: The Junk-bond Raiders and the Man Who Staked Them*, New York: Simon and Schuster.

Bureau of Economic Analysis (2007), 'National income and product accounts,' accessed May 5, at www.bea.gov.

Business Week (2005), 'Corporate America's new Achilles' heel: overreliance on profits from finance units may be setting companies up for a fall,' **3926**, March 28.

Carpenter, R., S.M. Fazzari and B. Petersen (1995), 'Three financing constraint hypotheses and inventory investment: new tests with time and sectoral heterogeneity,' Economics Working Paper Archive Macroeconomics Series no: 9510001, accessed 29 October 2007 at http://129.3.20.41/eps/mac/papers/9510/ 9510001.pdf.

Carpenter, M., W. Lazonick, and M. O'Sullivan (2003), 'The stock market and innovative capability in the new economy: the optical networking industry,' *Industrial and Corporate Change*, **12** (5), 963–1034.

Chandler, A.D. (1977), *The Visible Hand: The Managerial Revolution in American Business*, Cambridge, MA: Harvard University Press.

Chernow, R. (1990), *The House of Morgan: An American Banking Dynasty and the Rise of Modern Finance*, New York: Atlantic Monthly Press.

Chirinko, R. (1993), 'Business fixed investment spending: empirical results, and policy implications,' *Journal of Economic Literature*, **31** (4), 1875–911.

Chirinko, R., S. Fazzari and A. Meyer (1999), 'How responsive is business capital formation to its user cost? An exploration with micro data,' *Journal of Public Economics*, **74**, 53–80.

Coleman, W. (1996), *Financial Services, Globalization and Domestic Policy Change. A Comparison of North America and the European Union*, Basingstoke: Macmillan.

Covert, J. and G. McWilliams (2006), 'At Sears, investing – not retail – drive profit,' *Wall Street Journal*, 17 November, p. C1.

Crotty, J. (1990), 'Owner-manager conflict and financial theory of investment stability: a critical assessment of Keynes, Tobin, and Minsky,' *Journal of Post Keynesian Economics*, **12** (4), 519–42.

Crotty, J. (1993), 'Rethinking Marxian investment theory: Keynes–Minsky instability, competitive regime shifts and coerced Investment,' *Review of Radical Political Economics* **25** (1), 1–26.

Crotty, J. (2000), 'Structural contradictions of the global neoliberal regime,' *Review of Radical Political Economics*, **32** (3), 361–8.

Crotty, J. (2002), 'The effects of increased product market competition and changes in financial markets on the performance of non-financial corporations in the neoliberal era,' Political Economy Research Institute working paper no. 44.

Crotty, J. (2005), 'The neoliberal paradox: the impact of destructive product market competition and "modern" financial markets on non-financial corporation performance in the neoliberal era,' in G. Epstein (ed.), *Financialization and the World Economy*, Cheltenham, UK and Northampton, MA, USA: Edward Elgar, pp. 77–110.

Crotty, J. (2007), 'If financial market competition is so intense, why are financial firm profits so high? Reflections on the current "Golden Age" of finance,' Political Economy Research Institute working paper no. 134.

Crotty, J. and J.P. Goldstein (1992), 'A Marxian–Keynesian theory of investment demand: empirical evidence,' in F. Moseley and E. Wolff (eds), *International Perspectives on Profitability and Accumulation*, Cheltenham, UK and Northampton, MA, USA: Edward Elgar, pp. 197–234.

Crotty, J. and D. Goldstein (1993), 'Do US financial markets allocate capital efficiently? The case of corporate restructuring in the 1980s,' in G. Dymski, G. Epstein and R. Pollin, (eds), *Transforming the US Financial System: Equity and Efficiency for the 21st Century*, Armonk, NY: M.E. Sharpe (for the Economic Policy Institute), pp. 253–86.

Crotty, J. and K. Lee (2005), 'Economic performance in post-crisis Korea: a critical perspective on neoliberal restructuring,' in G. Epstein (ed.), *Financialization and the World Economy*, Cheltenham, UK and Northampton, MA, USA: Edward Elgar, pp. 334–53.

D'Arista, J. (1994a), *The Evolution of US Finance*, vol 1, Armonk, NY: M.E. Sharpe.

D'Arista, J. (1994b), *The Evolution of US Finance*, vol 2, Armonk, NY: M.E. Sharpe.

D'Arista, J. (2005), 'The role of the international monetary system in financialization,' in G. Epstein (ed.), *Financialization and the World Economy*, Cheltenham, UK and Northampton, MA, USA: Edward Elgar, pp. 220–39.

Davis, E.P. and B. Steil (2001), *Institutional Investors*, Cambridge, MA: MIT Press.

Davis, G.F. and S.K. Stout (1992), 'Organization theory and the market for corporate control: a dynamic analysis of the characteristics of large takeover targets,' *Administrative Science Quarterly*, **37**, 605–33.

Davis, G.F. and T.A. Thompson (1994), 'A social movement perspective on corporate control,' *Administrative Science Quarterly*, **39** (1), 141–73.

De Long, J.B. (1991), 'Did J.P. Morgan's men add value? An economist's perspective on financial capitalism,' in P. Temin (ed.), *Inside the Business Enterprise: Historical Perspectives on the Use of Information*, Chicago: University of Chicago Press, pp. 205–36.

D'Eramo, M. (2003), *The Pig and the Skyscraper, Chicago: A History of Our Future*, London: Verso.

Dickens, Edwin (1998), 'Bank influence and the failure of US monetary policy during the 1953–54 recession,' *International Review of Applied Economics*, **28** (3), 115–25.

Donaldson, G. (1994), *Corporate Restructuring*, Boston, MA: Harvard Business School Press.

Dore, R. (2000), *Stock Market Capitalism: Welfare Capitalism*, New York: Oxford University Press.

Dore, R. (2002), 'Stock market capitalism and its diffusion,' *New Political Economy*, **7** (1), 115–21.

Downes, G.R. Jr., E. Houminer and R.G. Hubbard (1999), *Institutional Investors and Corporate Behavior*, Washington, DC: AEI Press.

Duesenberry, J.S. (1958), *Business Cycles and Economic Growth*, New York: McGraw Hill.

Dufour, M. and Ö. Orhangazi (2007a), 'International financial crises: scourge or blessing in disguise,' *Review of Radical Political Economics*, **39** (3), 342–50.

Dufour, M. and Ö. Orhangazi (2007b), 'The 2000–01 financial crises in Turkey: a crisis for whom?,' mimeo, Roosevelt University.

Duménil, G. and D. Lévy (2003), 'Periodizing capitalism. Technology, institutions, and relations of production,' accessed 9 September 2007 at www.jourdan.ens.fr/levy.

Duménil, G. and D. Lévy (2004a), *Capital Resurgent*, Cambridge, MA: Harvard University Press.

Duménil, G. and D. Lévy (2004b), 'The real and financial components of profitability (USA 1952–2000),' *Review of Radical Political Economics*, **36** (1), 82–110.

Duménil, G. and D. Lévy (2004c), 'Neoliberal income trends: wealth, class and ownership in the USA,' *New Left Review*, **30**, 105–33.

Duménil, G. and D. Lévy (2005), 'Costs and benefits of Neoliberalism: a class analysis,' in G. Epstein (ed.), *Financialization and the World Economy*, Cheltenham, UK and Northampton, MA, USA: Edward Elgar, pp. 17–45.

Dymski, G. (1991), 'From Schumpeterian credit flows to Minskian fragility: the transformation of the US banking system, 1927–1990,' mimeo, Department of Economics, University of Southern California.

Eichner, A. (1976), *Megacorp and Oligopoly: Micro Foundations of Macro Dynamics*, Cambridge: Cambridge University Press.

Eisinger, J. (2004), 'Interest rates, corporate profits,' *Wall Street Journal*, 9 February, p. C1.

Eisner, R. (1958), 'Expectation, plans, and capital expenditures: a synthesis of ex post and ex ante data,' in M. Bowman (ed.), *Expectations,*

Uncertainty, and Business Behavior, New York: Social Science Research Council, pp. 165–88.

Eisner, R. (1960), 'A distributed lag investment function,' *Econometrica*, **28**, 1–29.

Eisner, R. (1974), 'Econometric studies of investment behavior: a comment,' *Economic Inquiry*, **12** (1), 91–104.

Elliott, G., T. Rothenberg and J. Stock (1996), 'Efficient tests for an autoregressive unit root,' *Econometrica*, **64**, 813–36.

Engels, F. (1877), *Anti-Duhring*, reprinted 1976, Peking: Foreign Language Press.

Engen, E.M. and A. Lehnert (2000), 'Mutual funds and the US equity market,' *Federal Reserve Bulletin*, December, 797–812.

Epstein, G. (1994), 'A political economy model of comparative central banking,' in Gary Dymski and Robert Pollin (eds), *New Perspectives in Monetary Macroeconomics*, Ann Arbor, MI: University of Michigan Press.

Epstein, G. (2005), *Financialization and the World Economy*, Cheltenham, UK and Northampton, MA, USA: Edward Elgar.

Epstein, G. and A. Jayadev (2005), 'The rise of rentier incomes in OECD countries: financialization, central bank policy and labor solidarity,' in G. Epstein (ed.), *Financialization and the World Economy*, Cheltenham, UK and Northampton, MA, USA: Edward Elgar, pp. 46–74.

Epstein, G. and D. Power (2003), 'Rentier incomes and financial crises: an empirical examination of trends and cycles in some OECD countries,' *Canadian Journal of Development Studies*, **29** (2), 230–48.

Fama, E. and M. Jensen (1983a), 'Separation of ownership and control,' *Journal of Law and Economics*, **26**, 301–25.

Fama, E. and M. Jensen (1983b), 'Agency problems and residual claims,' *Journal of Law and Economics*, **26**, 327–49.

Farrell, D., S. Lund and A. Maasry (2007), *Mapping the Global Capital Market*, third annual report, New York: McKinsey Global Institute.

Fazzari, S. (1993), 'Monetary policy, financial structure and investment,' in G. Dymski, G. Epstein and R. Pollin (eds), *Transforming the US Financial System*, Armonk, NY: M.E. Sharpe, pp. 35–63.

Fazzari, S., R. Hubbard and B. Peterson (1988), 'Financing constraints and corporate investment,' *Brookings Papers on Economic Activity*, **1**, 141–95.

Federal Deposit Insurance Corporation (FDIC) (1997), *History of the 1980s: Lessons for the Future, Volume II: Symposium Proceedings*, Washington, DC: FDIC.

Federal Deposit Insurance Corporation (FDIC) (2007), 'Historical statistics on banking,' accessed May 5, at www.fdic.gov.

Federal Reserve (2007), 'Flow of funds accounts of the US,' accessed May 5, at www.federalreserve.gov.

Felix, D. (2005), 'Why international capital mobility should be curbed and how it could be done,' in G. Epstein (ed.), *Financialization and the World Economy*, Cheltenham, UK and Northampton, MA, USA: Edward Elgar, pp. 384–408.

Feng, H., J. Froud, S. Johal, C. Haslam and K. Williams (2001), 'A new business model? The capital market and the new economy,' *Economy and Society*, **30** (4), Nov: 467–503.

Fingleton, E. (1999), *In Praise of Hard Industries*, Boston, MA: Houghton Mifflin.

Fligstein, N. and L. Markowitz (1990), 'Financial reorganization of American corporations in the 1980s,' in W.J. Wilson (ed.), *Sociology and the Public Agenda*, Newbury Park, CA: Sage, pp. 185–206.

Foster, J.B. (2007), 'Financialization of capitalism,' *Monthly Review*, April, 1-12.

Froud, J., C. Haslam, S. Johal and K. William (2000), 'Shareholder value and financialization: consultancy promises, management moves,' *Economy and Society*, **29** (1), 80–110.

Froud, J., S. Johal and K. William (2002a), 'Financialization and the coupon pool,' *Capital and Class*, **78**, 119–51.

Froud, J., S. Johal and K. William (2002b), 'New agendas for auto research: financialization, motoring, and present day capitalism,' *Competition and Change*, **6** (1), 11.

Galbraith, J. (1967), *The New Industrial State*, New York: New American Library.

Gale, D. and M. Hellwig (1985), 'Incentive compatible debt contract: the one period problem,' *Review of Economic Studies*, **3**, 647–64.

Gaughan, P. (1996), *Mergers, Acquisitions, and Corporate Restructuring*, New York: John Wiley & Sons.

Gertler, M. and G. Gilchrist (1994), 'Monetary policy, business cycles, and the behavior of small manufacturing firms,' *Quarterly Journal of Economics*, **109** (2), 309–40.

Gillan, S. (2006), 'Recent developments in corporate governance: an overview,' *Journal of Corporate Finance*, **12**, 381–402.

Glen, J., K. Lee and A. Singh (2000), 'Competition, corporate governance and financing of corporate growth in emerging markets,' Cambridge University, Department of Applied Economics discussion paper in accounting and finance no AF46.

Goodhart, C.A.E. (1989), *Money, Information and Uncertainty*, Cambridge, MA: MIT Press.

Gowan, P. (1999), *The Global Gamble: Washington's Faustian Bid for World Dominance*, London and New York: Verso.

Grabel, I. (1997), 'Savings, investment, and functional efficiency: a comparative examination of national financial complexes,' in R. Pollin (ed.), *The Macroeconomics of Savings, Finance and Investment*, Ann Arbor, MI: University of Michigan Press, pp. 251–97.

Grabel, I. (2005), 'Averting crisis? Assessing measures to manage financial integration in emerging economies,' in G. Epstein (ed.), *Financialization and the World Economy*, Cheltenham, UK and Northampton, MA, USA: Edward Elgar, pp. 357–83.

Grahl, H. and P. Lysandrou (2006), 'Capital market trading volume: an overview and some preliminary conclusions,' *Cambridge Journal of Economics*, **30**, 955–79.

Grahl, J. and P. Teague (2000), 'The regulation school, the employment relation and financialization,' *Economy and Society*, **29** (1), 160–78.

Greene, W.H. (2003), *Econometric Analysis*, Englewood Cliffs, NJ: Prentice Hall.

Grossman, S. and O. Hart (1982), 'Corporate financial structure and managerial incentives,' in J. McCall (ed.), *The Economics of Information and Uncertainty*, Chicago: University of Chicago Press, pp. 107–40.

Grullon, G. and R. Michaely (2002), 'Dividends, share repurchases, and the substitution hypothesis,' *Journal of Finance*, **57** (4), 1649–84.

Hamilton, J. (1994), *Time Series Analysis*, Princeton, NJ: Princeton University Press.

Harvey, D. (1982), *The Limits to Capital*, London: Verso.

Harvey, D. (2003), *New Imperialism*, Oxford: Oxford University Press.

Harvey, D. (2005), *A Brief History of Neoliberalism*, Oxford: Oxford University Press.

Heilbroner, R. and A. Singer (1984), *The Economic Transformation of America: 1600 to the Present*, San Diego, CA: Harcourt Brace Jovanovich.

Henwood, D. (1997), *Wall Street*, New York: Verso.

Henwood, D. (2003), *After the New Economy*, New York: New Press.

Hilferding, R. (1910), *Finance Capital: A Study of the Latest Phase of Capitalist Development*, reprinted 1985, London and Boston: Routledge & Kegan Paul.

Holmstrom, B. and S.N. Kaplan (2001), 'Corporate governance and merger activity in the US: making sense of the 1980s and 1990s,' National Bureau for Economic Research working paper 8220.

Hudson, M. (2003), *Super Imperialism: The Origin and Fundamentals of US World Dominance*, London and Sterling, VA: Pluto Press.

IMF (International Monetary Fund) (2006), *Global Financial Stability Report: Market Developments and Issues*, April, Washington, DC: International Monetary Fund.

Isenberg, D. (2000), 'The political economy of financial reform: the origins of the US deregulation of 1980 and 1982,' in Robert Pollin (ed.),

Capitalism, Socialism, and Radical Political Economy, Cheltenham, UK and Northampton, MA, USA: Edward Elgar, pp. 247–69.

Jensen, M. (2003), 'The agency cost of overvalued equity,' *CESifo Forum*, 14–16.

Jensen, M. and W. Meckling (1976), 'Theory of the firm: managerial behavior, agency costs and capital structure,' *Journal of Financial Economics*, **3**, 11–25.

Jones, G. (2005), 'Multinationals from the 1930 to the 1980s,' in Alfred D. Chandler Jr. and Bruce Mazlish (eds), *Leviathans: Multinational Corporations and the New Global History*, Cambridge: Cambridge University Press, pp. 81–103.

Jorgenson, D.W. (1971), 'Econometric studies of investment behavior: a survey,' *Journal of Economic Literature*, **53**, 1111–47.

Jürgens, U., K. Naumann and J. Rupp (2000), 'Shareholder value in an adverse environment: the German case,' *Economy and Society*, **29** (1), 54–79.

Jürgens, U., Y. Lung, G. Volpato and V. Frigant (2002), 'The arrival of shareholder value in the European auto industry: a case study comparison of four car makers,' *Competition and Change*, **6** (1), 61–80.

Kaplan, C., E. Özmen and C. Yalçın (2006), 'The determinants and implications of financial asset holdings of non-financial firms in Turkey: an empirical investigation,' The Central Bank of the Republic of Turkey Research and Monetary Policy Department working paper no. 06/06.

Khemani, R.S. and D.M. Shapiro (1993), *Glossary of Industrial Organization Economics and Competition Law*, Paris: Directorate for Financial, Fiscal and Enterprise Affairs, OECD.

Khoury, S. (1990), *The Deregulation of the World Financial Markets: Myths, Realities, and Impact*, New York: Quorum Books.

Kopcke, R. with R. Brauman (2001), 'The performance of traditional macroeconomic models of businesses' investment spending,' *New England Economic Review*, **2**, 3–39.

Kotz, D. (2003), 'Neoliberalism and the social structure of accumulation theory of long-run capital accumulation,' *Review of Radical Political Economics*, **35**, 263–70.

Kotz, D. (2007), 'Social structures of accumulation and the rate of capital accumulation: a revised understanding of the SSA theory,' mimeo, University of Massachusetts Amherst.

Krippner, G. (2005), 'The financialization of the American economy,' *Socio-Economic Review*, **3** (2), 173–208.

Kuh, E. (1963), 'Theory of institutions in the study of investment behavior,' *American Economic Review*, **53** (2), 260–8.

Kuh, E. and J. Meyer (1955), 'Acceleration and related theories of invest-
   ment: an empirical inquiry,' *Review of Economics and Statistics*, **38** (3):
   217–30.
Kuttner, R. (1997), *Everything For Sale*, New York: Alfred A. Knopf.
Lavoie, M. (1992), *Foundations of Post-Keynesian Econometric Analysis*,
   Aldershot, UK and Brookfield, US: Edward Elgar.
Lazonick, W. and M. O'Sullivan (1997), 'Investment in innovation, cor-
   porate governance and corporate employment,' *Jerome Levy Economics
   Institute policy brief no. 37.*
Lazonick, W. and M. O'Sullivan (2000), 'Maximizing shareholder value: a
   new ideology for corporate governance,' *Economy and Society*, **29** (1),
   13–35.
Lease, R.C., K. John, A. Kalay, U. Loewenstein and O.H. Sarig (2000),
   Dividend Policy, Boston, MA: Harvard Business School Press.
Lenin, V. (1916), *Imperialism, The Highest Stage of Capitalism: A Popular
   Outline*, reprinted 1988, New York: International Publishers.
Lowenstein, R. (2004), *Origins of the Crash: The Great Bubble and Its
   Undoing*, Harmondsworth: Penguin Books.
Luxemburg, R. (1968), *The Accumulation of Capital*, New York: Monthly
   Review Press.
Magdoff, H. and P.M. Sweezy (1987), *Stagnation and Financial Explosion*,
   New York: Monthly Review Press.
Marglin, S. and A. Bhaduri (1990), 'Profit squeeze and Keynesian theory,'
   in S. Marglin and J. Schor (eds), *The Golden Age of Capitalism*, Oxford:
   Clarenden Press, pp. 81–103.
Markham, J.W. (2002), *A Financial History of the United States*, vol II, New
   York: M.E. Sharpe.
Martin, R. (2002), *Financialization of Daily Life*, Philadelphia, PA: Temple
   University Press.
Mayer, C. (1988), 'New issues in corporate finance,' *European Economic
   Review*, **32**, 1167–89.
Medoff, J. and A. Harless (1996), *The Indebted Society*, Boston, MA: Little,
   Brown.
Minsky, H. (1975), *John Maynard Keynes*, New York: Columbia University
   Press.
Minsky, H. (1986), *Stabilizing an Unstable Economy*, New Haven, CT: Yale
   University Press.
Mitchell, M. and H. Mulherin (1996), 'The impact of industry shocks on
   takeover and restructuring activity,' *Journal of Financial Economics*, **41**
   (2), 193–229.
Moffitt, D. (1983), *The American Character: Views of America from the
   Wall Street Journal*, New York: G. Braziller.

Morin, F. (2000), 'A transformation in the French model of shareholding and management,' *Economy and Society*, **29** (1), 36–53.

New York Stock Exchange (2007), 'NYSE factbook of historical statistics,' accessed May 5, at www.nyse.com.

Ndikumana, L. (1999), 'Debt service, financing constraints, and fixed investment: evidence from panel data,' *Journal of Post Keynesian Economics*, **21** (3), 455–78.

Ndikumana, L. (2005), 'Financial development, financial structure, and domestic investment: international evidence,' *Journal of International Money and Finance*, **24**, 651–73.

O'Connell, A. (2005), 'The Argentine financial crisis,' in G. Epstein (ed.), *Financialization and the World Economy*, Cheltenham, UK and Northampton, MA, USA: Edward Elgar, pp. 289–313.

O'Sullivan, M. (2000), *Contests for Corporate Control: Corporate Governance and Economic Performance in the United States and Germany*, Oxford: Oxford University Press.

Organisation for Economic Co-operation and Development (OECD) (1998), 'Shareholder value and the market in corporate control in OECD countries,' *Financial Market Trends*, **69**, 15–38.

Panitch, L. and S. Gindin (2004), 'Finance and American Empire,' in L. Panitch and S. Gindin (eds), *Social Register 2005: The Empire Reloaded*, London: Merlin Press, pp. 46–81.

Panitch, L. and S. Gindin (2005), 'Superintending global capital,' *New Left Review*, (September–October), 101–23.

Parenteau, R. (2005), 'The late 1990s US bubble: financialization in the extreme,' in G. Epstein (ed.), *Financialization and the World Economy*, Cheltenham, UK and Northampton, MA, USA: Edward Elgar, pp. 111–48.

Perry, K. and R. Taggart (1988), 'The growing role of junk bonds in corporate finance,' *Journal of Applied Corporate Finance*, **37** (45), 37–45.

Phillips, K. (2006), *American Theocracy*, New York: Viking.

Pineault, E. (2001), 'Finance capital and the institutional foundations of capitalist finance: theoretical elements from Marx to Minsky,' unpublished paper, Ecole des Hautes Etudes en Sciences Sociales, Paris.

Pollin, R. (1996), 'Contemporary economic stagnation in world historical perspective,' *New Left Review*, (September–October), 109–18.

Power, D., G. Epstein and M. Abrena (2003), 'Trends in rentier incomes in OECD countries: estimates, data and methods,' mimeo, University of Massachusetts Amherst Political Economy Research Institute.

Ramirez, C.D. (1995), 'Did J.P. Morgan's men add liquidity? Corporate investment, cash flow, and financial structure at the turn of the twentieth century,' *Journal of Finance*, **1** (2), 661–78.

Roberts, D. (2006), 'Opposition grows to earnings forecasts,' *Financial Times*, 13 March, p. 1.

Rosenberg, S. and T. Weisskopf (1981), 'A conflict theory approach to inflation in the postwar US economy,' *American Economic Review*, **71**, 42–7.

Ross, S. (1977), 'The determination of financial structure: the incentive-signaling approach,' *Bell Journal of Economics*, **3**, 458–82.

Russell, E. (2005), 'The contradictory imperatives of new deal banking reforms,' PhD thesis for the University of Massachusetts Amherst.

Schaberg, M. (1999), *Globalization and the Erosion of National Financial Systems*, Cheltenham, UK, Northampton, MA, USA: Edward Elgar.

Schleifer, A. and R. Vishny (1997), 'A survey of corporate governance,' *Journal of Finance*, **52**, 737–83.

Schumpeter, J. (1934 [1961]), *Theory of Economic Development: An Inquiry into Profits, Capital, Credit, Interest and the Business Cycle*, Cambridge, MA: Harvard University Press.

Seccombe, W. (2004), 'Contradictions of shareholder capitalism, downsizing jobs, enlisting savings, destabilizing families,' in L. Panitch, C. Leys, A. Zuege and M. Konings (eds), *The Globalization Decade: A Critical Reader*, London: Merlin Press, pp. 193–220.

Singh, A. (2003), 'Competition, corporate governance and selection in emerging markets,' *Economic Journal*, **113** (491), F443–F464.

Soederberg, S. (2003), 'The promotion of "Anglo-American" corporate governance in the south: who benefits from the new international standard?', *Third World Quarterly*, **24** (1), 7–27.

Stock, J. and M. Watson (2003), *Introduction to Econometrics*, Reading, MA: Addison-Wesley.

Stockhammer, E. (2004), 'Financialization and the slowdown of accumulation,' *Cambridge Journal of Economics*, **28**, 719–41.

Sweezy, P. (1997), 'More (or less) on globalization,' *Monthly Review*, **49** (4), 1–4.

Tainio, R. (2003), 'Financialization of key finnish companies,' *Nordiske Organisasjons-Studier*, **5** (2), 61–86.

Tobin, J. (1965), 'Money and economic growth,' *Econometrica*, **33**, 671–84.

Tobin, J. (1984), 'On the efficiency of the financial system,' Hirsch Memorial Lecture, New York, May 15.

Tobin, J. (1997), Comment, in R. Pollin (ed.), *The Macroeconomics of Savings, Finance and Investment*, Ann Arbor, MI: University of Michigan Press.

Toporowski, J. (2000), *The End of Finance: the Theory of Capital Market Inflation, Financial Derivatives, and Pension Fund Capitalism*, London, New York: Routledge.

Townsend, R. (1979), 'Optimal contracts and competitive markets with costly state verification,' *Journal of Economic Theory*, **21**, 265–93.

Useem, M. (1996), *Investor Capitalism: How Money Managers are Changing the Face of Corporate America*, New York: Basic Books.

Wade, H. Robert (2005), 'The march of neoliberalism and what to do about it,' draft paper for plenary talk at conference Beyond 'Deregulation': Finance in the 21st Century, University of Sussex, 26-28 May 2005.

Weller, C. and B. Helppie (2002), 'Did the stock market boom of the late 1990s impede investment in manufacturing?', Economic Policy Institute technical paper, Washington, DC.

White House (2007), *Economic Report of the President Transmitted to the Congress February 2007*, Washington, DC: US Government Printing Office.

Williams, K. (2000), 'From shareholder value to present day capitalism,' *Economy and Society*, **29** (1), 1–12.

Wolfson, M.H. (1994), *Financial Crises: Understanding the Postwar US Experience*, Armonk, NY: M.E. Sharpe.

Wolfson, M. (2003), 'Neoliberalism and the social structure of accumulation,' *Review of Radical Political Economics*, **35**, 255–62.

Index

152 *Index*

financial transactions 3, 8, 11, 13, 22,
    82, 88
financialization
    and capital accumulation 87–94, 98,
        104–5, 127, 130–31
    and investment 99–128, *see also*
        financialization and capital
        accumulation
    causes and consequences of 71–5
    definitions 3–6, 11
    literature on 6–8, 41–71
    of NFCs 11, 15–22, 32, 74–5
financing constraint 96, 126
Fingleton, E. 4
Fligstein, N. 89
firms
    financial 24, 33, 64, 118, *see also*
        financial businesses; financial
        corporations
    small 119–20, 122, 126
    large 22, 117, 123, 125–7, 130
    manufacturing 61, 120, 123, 125
    non-manufacturing 119–20, 123, 130
fiscal policy 50
Ford Credit Company 32
France 7, 58, 69–71, 91
Froud, J. 7, 41, 62, 63, 65, 66, 92

Galbraith, J. 93
Gale, D. 62
Gaughan, P. 37
General Motors Acceptance
    Corporation (GMAC)
gentleman bankers' code 24
Germain Act 2
Germany 19, 24–5, 27, 69–71
Gillan, S. 38, 62, 132
Gindin, S. 41, 56, 58, 59, 73
Glass-Steagall 29, 33
Glen, J. 7, 62
globalization 3, 6, 52, 58, 68
Golden Age 9, 28–31, 51, 69
Goldstein, J. 60, 93
Goodhart, C. 29
Gowan, P. 34, 56
Grahl, H. 14

Grabel, I. 8
Great Depression 28–9, 55, 73
Grossman, S. 62

Hamilton, J. 102
Hansen-Sargan test 122, 124
Harless, A. 34
Hart, O. 62
Harvey, D. 7, 34, 41, 49, 51, 55–58, 72
hedge funds 57, 132
hegemony 43–6, 48, 51, 54, 56, 73
    crisis of 42, *see also* hegemonic crisis
hegemonic crisis 43, 45
Heilbroner, R. 24
Hellwig, M. 62
Helppie, B. 60
Henwood, D. 7
Hilferding, R. 24–5, 41, 43
Holmstorm, B. 32, 35, 37, 38
hostile takeover *see* takeover
household 65, 67
    borrowing 67
    debt 50, 73
Hudson, M. 56
hybrid financial institutions 32

International Monetary Fund (IMF)
    16, 50, 57, 131
imperialism (imperialist) 43, 57
income distribution 7–8, 58, 132
income inequality 7, 45
inflation 30–31, 39, 48, 55
    asset price 52, 54
insurance companies 13, 32, 37, 64, 90
institutional investors 34–7, 40, 50, 63,
    65–6, 74–5, 87, 89, 90
interest
    income 13, 48–9, 82–3, 100–101,
        120, 126
    expense 120
    payments 6, 7, 19–20, 81–3. 85, 87,
        89–91, 100, 118, 126, 129, 130
    rates 19, 29–31, 49–50, 55, 60, 73, 93
internal funds 9, 59, 82, 85–8, 93–6,
    118
internationalization 30, 33, 70

NEW DIRECTIONS IN MODERN ECONOMICS

Post-Keynesian Monetary Economics
New Approaches to Financial Modelling
Edited by Philip Arestis

Keynes's Principle of Effective Demand
Edward J. Amadeo

New Directions in Post-Keynesian Economics
Edited by John Pheby

Theory and Policy in Political Economy
Essays in Pricing, Distribution and Growth
Edited by Philip Arestis and Yiannis Kitromilides

Keynes's Third Alternative?
The Neo-Ricardian Keynesians and the Post Keynesians
Amitava Krishna Dutt and Edward J. Amadeo

Wages and Profits in the Capitalist Economy
The Impact of Monopolistic Power and Macroeconomic Performance in
the USA and UK
Andrew Henley

Prices, Profits and Financial Structures
A Post-Keynesian Approach to Competition
Gokhan Capoglu

International Perspectives on Profitability and Accumulation
Edited by Fred Moseley and Edward N. Wolff

Mr Keynes and the Post Keynesians
Principles of Macroeconomics for a Monetary Production Economy
Fernando J. Cardim de Carvalho

The Economic Surplus in Advanced Economies
Edited by John B. Davis

Foundations of Post-Keynesian Economic Analysis
Marc Lavoie

The Post-Keynesian Approach to Economics
An Alternative Analysis of Economic Theory and Policy
Philip Arestis

Sustainable Fiscal Policy and Economic Stability
Theory and Practice
Philippe Burger

The Rise of Unemployment in Europe
A Keynesian Approach
Engelbert Stockhammer

General Equilibrium, Capital, and Macroeconomics
A Key to Recent Controversies in Equilibrium Theory
Fabio Petri

Post-Keynesian Principles of Economic Policy
Claude Gnos and Louis-Philippe Rochon

Innovation, Evolution and Economic Change
New Ideas in the Tradition of Galbraith
Blandine Laperche, James K. Galbraith and Dimitri Uzunidis

The Economics of Keynes
A New Guide to *The General Theory*
Mark Hayes

Money, Distribution and Economic Policy
Alternatives to Orthodox Macroeconomics
Edited by Eckhard Hein and Achim Truger

Modern State Intervention in the Era of Globalisation
Nikolaos Karagiannis and Zagros Madjd-Sadjadi

Financialization and the US Economy
Özgür Orhangazi